THE
POWER
OF
HEX

THE POWER OF HEX

SPELLS, INCANTATIONS, AND RITUALS

SHAWN ENGEL

CHICAGO
REVIEW
PRESS

CONTENTS

THE POWER OF HEX

Welcome to The Power of Hex*! Reading this book is the first step in reclaiming your power and strength in a world that needs leaders and heroes. If you are a witch interested in activism and protecting those in the margins, you have come to the right place.*

Hexing gets a bad rap for a multitude of reasons. For one, just as there are non-practitioners with poor intentions that wish ill on others, there are witches who do the same. While we can't control everyone or demonize a practice just because of a few bad apples, we can make a personal effort to approach the practice with caution.

There is a lot of misinformation about hexing, cursing, and jinxing, so this book aims to educate you on the "who," "what," and mainly the "why" of hexing. When we define exactly why a hex is necessary, we not only strengthen the effectiveness of our magic, but we also help to clarify our own morality. This is a very important step in practicing magic. Even witches have to live with the consequences of their choices, so always practice according to your moral code.

This book will simplify hexing and empower you to use this magical tool with accountability. Beginning by defining hexing, unpacking the ethics of hexing, and showing you how disenfranchised groups have used this type of magic for protection throughout history, I will then lead into modern takes on the practice. From there, an overview of focusing energy in different rituals will branch off into into four main spell chapters, finishing with a chapter dedicated to building your own spells using aligned ingredients.

This book aims to simplify this powerful type of magic while enforcing morality. We don't want to sink to the level of those we are cursing; hexing is meant to protect and arm.

IF YOU ARE READY TO TAKE THE JOURNEY, LET'S DIVE IN!

1

THE
WORLD
OF
HEXING

Hexing is a form of magic that should be taken seriously and approached with caution and respect. Not only can you use hexing to access the power you hold within yourself, achieve self-empowerment, influence the world around you, and exert control over your life, but also to help others who cannot protect themselves.

WHAT IS HEXING?

Hexing is one of the oldest forms of magic. Hexe *is the German word for* witch, *and it can, in fact, be difficult to separate hexing from witchcraft. People often mistakenly associate hexing with cursing, baneful spells, and wishing ill on others, but when cast by a responsible witch, hexing is a form of protection, rather than harm.*

Modern witches are often asked naive questions such as "Do you curse people?" or "Have you ever hexed?" I believe that questions like these largely stem from the misguided notion that all witches are evil and so should be feared. This fear goes back centuries and, as I explain in more detail later, witches have long been persecuted for their practices. In the past, if they held on to what they believed in—by refusing to confess to the practice of witchcraft, for example—they would be punished in some way, such as being beaten, burned at the stake, crushed with heavy rocks, or thrown into rivers. These punishments were a response to a collective fear that witches were more powerful than those in authority. Such a response has been seen countless times across different cultures, periods, and countries throughout history. Notable examples include the persecution and punishment of witches across Europe in the Middle Ages and in Salem, Massachusetts, in the late 17th century.

"IF YOU CAN'T HEX, YOU CAN'T HEAL"

People's fear of hexing has always intrigued me, but I think it actually reveals a curiosity to learn more about these mysterious practices. This fear also stems from the fact that most people do not understand exactly what hexing is or why it is used. And, no, it is not meant to be used as a way of attacking or hurting anyone that displeases you. Instead, it should be regarded as a form of self-defense and protection—much like karate or jiujitsu, but in the spiritual realm.

There is a very old expression in witchcraft: "If you can't hex, you can't heal." This basically means that, to begin healing, you must first protect yourself and rid your environment of oppression, a process that can manifest itself in many different ways. So, essentially, for our purposes, this phrase highlights that you may need to use hexing to defend yourself first before you can begin that healing process. This might mean removing someone from your energetic sphere, for example, as a means of self-defense, so you can continue minding your own business and start working on yourself.

Indeed, hexing is helpful for those seeking to deal with difficult personal situations or who want more control over their lives. You can also use hexing to protect yourself from curses, psychic attacks, and those who wish you harm. Not only can hexing be used in interpersonal relationships—to remove a toxic person or influence from your life, for example—but also on a larger scale, such as the recent mass hexing of Brett Kavanaugh (see page 22).

GETTING STARTED

There is a temptation among beginning witches to use hexing purely for petty personal gain and vengeance. I cannot stress enough how ill advised this is. Though many of us may not believe in karma or the Rule of Three (see pages 32–33), there is still an overarching ethical stance in hexing, just as there is against hurting someone physically. The intention behind your hex must be pure and of the highest good, rather than reactionary and the result of anger directed toward someone you feel has wronged you. My advice is never to hex in the heat of the moment; instead, think through the possible consequences of every hex. Always examine the motives behind your spellwork and avoid sending out intentions that could affect others negatively. Remember, you need to be able to sleep soundly with a clear conscience based on your daily choices.

All of these issues will become clearer as you read through the book, but the key thing to remember is that with hexing—as with everything in this world—nothing is purely black or white. The gray area is where the magic lies, and hexing bends and amplifies the grayscale. Interestingly, the word *witch* is derived from the old Teutonic word *wik*, meaning *to bend*.

Bear in mind that hexes and spells cannot fix all the problems you may want them to, and that casting spells and hexing take both time and energy, as well as hard work and concentration. Also remember that this magic is powerful and playing with its power calls for responsibility. This book provides clear guidance on the ethical and moral choices that should underpin hexing, but always treat your intentions like a loaded gun and respect the power that it holds when you pull the trigger.

ORIGINS

Hexing is as old as time and has been practiced for centuries by a variety of cultures to safeguard their beliefs and as a means of protection. This overview shows how and why hexing has been used at key moments in history, including in the ancient world, by indigenous tribes facing invasion by settlers, and by enslaved people from Africa.

THE ANCIENT WORLD

As long as humans have believed in gods, the supernatural world, and magic, spells and curses have been widely used. We are still fascinated by such practices, as seen by the huge popularity of movies like *The Curse of the Mummy* and the Harry Potter series. Hexing and spells were used by the ancient civilizations of Egypt, Greece, and Rome. Ancient Greeks and Romans used spells to control the outcome of sports events, business endeavors, and even love affairs. Such "binding" spells relied on set formats and phrases, spoken to achieve the results that were wanted. Spells were also written down. A 2,000 year old grave was recently unearthed near an ancient Roman city in Serbia, and tiny scrolls containing binding spells were found among the skeletons. Such amulets would have been carried around until the spells came to pass. Ancient Greek and Roman people often paid magicians to create these talismanic scrolls for them.

Also popular were curse tablets, made from lead, stone, or wax, on which people cursed those who they felt had harmed them in some way. The tablets would invoke the gods to bring down a curse on a specific person. Recently, 30 small lead tablets engraved with curses invoking the gods of the underworld were discovered at the bottom of a 2,500-year-old well in Athens, Greece. Another option was to take revenge on someone using a curse doll,

THE ANCIENT EGYPTIANS WERE INDEED QUITE MAGICAL, EVEN PRACTICING GLAMOUR MAGIC BY ENCHANTING PRECIOUS EMERALDS, GRINDING THEM UP, AND USING THE RESULTING POWDER AS EYESHADOW.

with examples having been found that had bound hands and feet. These dolls were probably used in association with a binding spell.

Spells and curses were also used in ancient Egypt, often woven into written stories. The ancient Egyptians were indeed quite magical, even practicing glamour magic by enchanting precious emeralds, grinding them up, and using the resulting powder as eyeshadow. Given their belief in the power of magic, it is no surprise that Egyptian rulers would put a protective hex in the tombs of the dead, so as to keep out raiders and thieves. This practice led to rumors that anyone who dares enter such a tomb would be cursed forever. As these stories passed down through history, they evolved to become much scarier and more macabre.

EUROPE

Witchcraft and the world of magic flourished in medieval Europe, but by early 17th century superstition began to surround witches, with neighborhoods blaming them for local disasters and difficulties. Although the Church initially dismissed such superstitions as pagan, a fear of witches persisted and, in 1484, Pope Innocent VIII proclaimed witchcraft to be heresy. This declaration encouraged

religious groups in Europe to begin persecuting witches. In 1486, a German clergyman published a book called the *Malleus Maleficarum* (*The Hammer of Witches*), which was essentially a guide to witch-hunting, while in England the 1542 Witchcraft Act made witchcraft and the casting of spells punishable by death (a law that was renewed in 1562 and 1604).

So began a period of widespread accusation, persecution, and execution throughout Europe that mainly targeted poor and middle-aged and elderly women. Such people would have struggled to survive and probably turned to witchcraft, spell-casting, and curses in order to fulfill their basic needs, whether this was simply for food and shelter, or for self-protection, personal justice, or revenge. As punishment for their craft, most witches were hanged, although in Scotland and Spain (under the jurisdiction of the Spanish Inquisition), some witches were burned at the stake, resulting in a period known as the Burning Times. It is estimated that from 1482 to 1782, some 100,000 people—mainly women—were accused of witchcraft and around 50,000 were executed after being found guilty during the witch trials. In the UK, the three main witch-hunts took place in East Lothian, Scotland (1590s), Lancashire (1612), and Essex and East Anglia (1640s). The first of these, the North Berwick witch trials, began in 1590 and lasted for two years. Those on trial were accused of practicing witchcraft in St Andrew's Auld Kirk in North Berwick. The accused witches were tortured until they confessed, whereupon they were executed.

AFRICA AND THE AMERICAS

Using curses and hexes as a form of protection has been common among various indigenous and native tribes through the centuries, mainly against white Christian settlers and slave traders. From the 16th through the 19th centuries, the transatlantic slave trade benefited the American colonies as slave traders looked to Africa in search of labor to exploit.

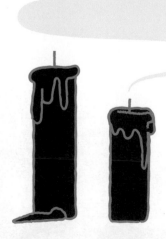

In response, native peoples used witchcraft and hexing as protective measures against those who invaded and pillaged their lands or forcibly removed them from their homes. Such acts were among the very few ways in which they could assert some form of power and show their resistance. They would use raw materials from the earth to ward off attacks and fashioned protective garb from animal parts. Snakeskin, for example, was often used to protect, while animal teeth and blood would cause harm to those who came near. The enslaved Africans taken from their homeland during this time period would work magic against their captors in order to protect themselves from physical abuse. Of course, the enslaved people could not practice openly, for fear of punishment, so their magic was kept hidden.

This need for protection led to the development of hoodoo, a folk-magic tradition created by enslaved African people in the New World, which focuses on the energy found in roots, herbs, crystals, and animals. Hoodoo uses magic to draw on those energies and match the intention behind the spell. What we think of today as voodoo dolls were originally intended as a means of protection against a slave master. It is also a little-known fact that the dolls are also meant to serve as aids to friends and family. Where a pin might appear, instead a balm or herb is placed to heal a wound. This shows clearly how hexing and healing can become one and the same.

A variety of hexing traditions were used in Salem, Massachusetts, but not always by those you'd expect. Focusing on poppets (tiny effigies of people), blood letting, and curse jars, every house in Salem had some sort of protective ward inside. And, quite often, townsfolk would repeat incantations to keep them safe from punishment or from "evil" witchcraft. The infamous Salem witch trials between February 1692 and May 1693 began after a group of young girls in Salem Village, Massachusetts, claimed to be possessed by the devil and accused several local women of witchcraft. This grew into a crowd frenzy that flung accusations at those who were perceived to be different.

You may also have heard of another tradition called powwow. This is a type of folk magic that uses charms and rituals to heal people and livestock, as well as to protect and bring good luck. Although powwow is a Native American term, the tradition was originally brought to the Pennsylvanian colonies during the migration of German-speaking settlers from Europe in the 17th and 18th centuries. It is thought that the Pennsylvanian tradition of painting hex signs, a type of folk art, is related to this powwow tradition. Usually round and decorated with colorful, geometric patterns, hex signs were used to shield communities from disasters such as war or natural calamities and, on a smaller scale, to protect farm animals from disease. They were also used to promote healing and abundance, rather than purely as a limiting barrier against negative outside forces.

Having looked at these few examples of witchcraft and spell-casting through the ages, it is clear that, although curiosity and fear around hexing may be warranted, such practices have mainly been used as a form of self defense and protection, rather than to harm another.

FOLKLORE AND MYTHOLOGY

*Similar to the tradition of moral storytelling, hexing has long been
used to illustrate consequences. In mythology, hexing or cursing is
put in place to protect, set a certain standard, or merely wish ill will
on another being, resulting in grand supernatural occurrences or
sometimes even death.*

ANCIENT EGYPT

The most notorious of hexes in folklore is, of course, the curse of the pharaohs. Whether in movies such as *The Mummy's Curse* (1944) and *The Mummy* (1999), or even in episodes of the TV series *The Simpsons*, most of us are familiar with the notion of ancient Egyptian curses that may fall on anyone who disturbs an Egyptian mummy. Indeed, hexing and cursing are often equated with ancient Egyptian culture. In an Egyptian tomb, the curse ensured that, whether through thievery or excavation, anyone who entered would fall ill or even die. Ominous inscriptions have been found inside the tombs of various Egyptian pharaohs and high-standing officials. For example, the tomb of a 10th Dynasty provincial governor called Ankhtifi, at El-Mo'Alla in Upper Egypt, contained the etched inscription stating that "anyone who shall do any wickedness in this coffin may not be allowed to offer any goods to Hemen and will not inherit, nor his heirs." To summarize another inscription found in the tomb of Khentika Ikhehi, who was also of the 10th Dynasty: "anyone who shall enter with impure intentions shall be judged with an end made, and I shall seize his neck like a bird and cast fear into him."

So, the Egyptians were evidently determined to protect the tombs of key figures of the time using curses. Although this might sound ominous, the ritual of inscribing the tombs with curses was again simply a means of protection. Interestingly, it is thought that this energy has carried through to modern times, with some archaeologists reporting illnesses and accidents after having entered a cursed tomb. These curses cannot be undone, as the pharaohs ordered the inscriptions and the curses remain.

ANCIENT OLYMPICS

As we have seen, curses were also widely used in ancient Greece. During the early Olymic Games, using hexing to win in the competition was frowned upon. Such malpractice was taken very seriously and competing athletes were expected to gather in front of a statue of Zeus to swear an oath that they would not use foul play to win, whether by bribing judges or doing something to impede their opponents. They were also forbidden from practicing black magic as a means of winning. Ironically, the competitors were also faced with a stone tablet stating that anyone who broke his oath would be cursed. The curse tablet called upon Zeus to smite anyone into ashes who disobeyed this rule and used curses to win, thus condemning a hex with a hex. Despite the warning, contestants would still use curses calling upon certain gods and goddesses to cripple their opponents, and they believed that these curses worked. The curses would be etched on tablets and placed under the floor or ground where the competition was to take place. Some participants in the games would cast a binding spell to debilitate a fellow competitor or, even worse, use magic calling for their death. During the games, if a competitor fell ill and could not take part, the watching crowd would assume that a hex had been placed on them.

JEWISH KABBALAH

In the Jewish faith, or more specifically in Kabbalah (the Jewish mystical tradition), we find the ancient curse of the Pulsa diNura. This is a ceremonial ritual performed to invoke the angels of destruction to block the subject from receiving any heavenly forgiveness, and often results in death. It is extremely controversial for obvious reasons, but the Pulsa diNura has been suggested as the reason behind the unexplained recent deaths of Israeli politicians, namely those of prime ministers Yitzhak Rabin in November 1995 and Ariel Sharon in 2006. This is merely a form of modern folklore following the frenzy of rumors circulating after the deaths of these politicians. The idea of shrouded rabbis casting curses is in actual fact a result of an old excommunication edict that has been blown out of proportion. And yet again, we see the purpose behind hexing being misconstrued by frightened people and stoked by the media.

EUROPEAN FOLKLORE

Folklore involving cursing and hexing can also be found in Europe. One promient piece of Italian folklore centers around the concept of *il malocchio* (evil eye). Put simply, it's the look that someone gives you when they are envious of what you have or have done. It is said that such a glance will cause bad luck, whether it is intentional or not. Many witches believe strongly in the power of the evil eye to this day, which is why many practitioners are known to wear evil-eye wards as jewelry.

To take another European example, in Irish mythology we find the story of the beautiful maiden Étaín who falls in love with Midir of Tuatha Dé Danann and becomes the victim of a series of curses by his scorned and rejected wife Fúamnach. Instead of moving on with her own life, Fúamnach becomes enraged and jealous of Midir's newfound love and devotes her time to ruining Étaín. First, she turns Étaín into a pool of water, then a worm, and then a fly. However, even as a fly, Étaín never leaves Midir's side and he remains completely unattracted to other women. Frustrated and vengeful, Fúamnach then conjures a wind that banishes Étaín to the rocks of the sea for seven years. Étaín finds herself saved from the sea but is then cast away again by Fúamnach many times over, thus showing a cycle of struggle, death, and rebirth.

You can see here how love spells and hexing can run parallel with each other. Because of her blind rage and inability to let go, Fúamnach sacrificed her whole life in her determination to ruin Étaín's. Clearly, anyone attempting a hex should heed this story.

RECENT HEXES

Witchcraft, magic, and hexing have all seeped into modern culture, as is seen from the popularity of TV series such as Charmed *and also the Harry Potter books. This modern view of witchcraft in popular culture has led such practices to be regarded more positively.*

Witchcraft and hexing are very much alive in today's world. They help many young people feel a sense of self-empowerment, giving them the belief that they can control their own lives and even influence the world around them. This has been seen most notably in the recent use of hexes in the world of politics. In the United States, hexing made the news after Donald Trump was elected as president. In 2016 witches across America rose up in protest and demanded the hexing of Trump. A social media hashtag #MagicResistance called for thousands of witches online to bind Donald Trump from doing harm. The mass ritual took place at midnight on February 24, 2017.

Catland, a local witchcraft store in Brooklyn, also called for the binding of Trump, as well as that of Brett Kavanaugh following his nomination for Supreme Court judge in 2018. Kavanaugh was accused publicly of sexual assault, with celebrities including Lana Del Rey calling for both Trump and Kavanaugh to be bound. Also of recent note was the mass hexing by thousands of witches angry at the lenient six-month sentence given to Brock Allen Turner, who was convicted of committing sexual assault in 2016.

These are all very modern examples of how witches use curses to exert their power in a world in which they feel justice isn't being done or their needs are not being met. What we're witnessing in this wave of recent hexes is a plea to the masses to focus their collective energy in order to achieve a desired outcome. In terms of "binding" (see Chapter 5), the intention behind such mass curses is to erect a barrier to prevent men in authority from creating an environment that is harmful to the American people. In many ways, these hexes may be viewed as an attack on the patriarchy.

TYPES OF HEXES

*There are four main types of hexes, with one protective ritual
that should be performed before practicing every hex.
This section covers the protective ritual and also the four hexes
in detail, with the ethics to consider alongside each one.*

PROTECTIVE RITUAL

What the ritual is While not a hex in itself, it is essential to practice protective magic before you even consider doing a hex. This type of work elevates your energy, which means that you may not even have to do the hex at all. This is the first stage in protecting yourself. To take the protection to the next level, it is necessary to move on to a binding or freezing spell.

When it is wise to use You should be using protective magic at all times to keep yourself safe from outside harm. This is as necessary as brushing your teeth or wearing your seatbelt while driving.

When not to use This is a very personal practice that affects no one negatively; instead, it serves to strengthen your own spirit. You can use it at all times.

BINDING SPELLS

What the hex is A binding spell keeps someone from doing harm to themselves or others. It keeps the subject of the spell in a stagnant state.

When it is wise to use In cases where the patriarchy is continuously performing malicious acts, for example, and other practical points of protection have been used, a binding spell is often appropriate.

When not to use If the target is merely inconvenient, rather than cruel. Free will is at question here, so binding should be a last resort.

FREEZING SPELLS

What the hex is Much like binding spells, a freezing spell stops the subject in its tracks. Performed with jars or frozen liquid, it is an another way to keep a perpetrator from doing harm.

When it is wise to use When the patriarchy is performing acts that make the witch or magician feel unsafe, after other avenues have been followed (such as voting and activism).

When not to use As with binding spells, if the nuisance is not of immediate threat or danger. This again compromises free will.

BANISHING SPELLS
What the hex is A banishing spell sends the subject of the spell away and ensures that they are unable to cause harm.

When it is wise to use If a person is continuously causing irreconcilable harm, and no other course of action is available to the witch/magician.

When not to use If the witch or magician merely disagrees with an opinion. Hexing should only be used in cases of an immediate threat, lest we play with the divine timing of fate.

HEALING SPELLS
What the hex is When a healing spell is cast on someone who did not request it, this is considered a hex because it manipulates free will.

When it is wise to use When the subject of the spell is causing unintended damage with their trauma.

When not to use When the threat is more immediate. Healing spells and their results tend to take longer to permeate a situation.

TO HEX OR NOT?

Deciding whether it is appropriate to hex in a given situation will help guide you along an ethical path. Drawing a line in the sand between petty upset and necessary measures will not only make you a better witch, but also a better person.

Whether a hex is necessary is something that you will feel in your gut, but there should always be a cooling-off period before you perform the hex. Taking an example from everyday life to illustrate this, consider some of the gun laws in the USA: a seven-day waiting period is imposed between the time you buy the gun and when you actually own it. This is intended to curb the potential for crimes of passion. Hexing calls for a similar self-imposed

waiting period. I know it may seem dramatic to compare hexing to gun ownership, but I can't stress enough how powerful the act of focused intention can be when it is backed up by rage. So, if you're a lover scorned who was just cheated on by her ex, take a breath before you hex.

To make the issue as clear as possible: when you are deciding whether or not to hex, consider the environment in which a hex may be appropriate. This approach should help you distinguish between actual oppression and merely something bad that has happened to you. It will take some dedication and forethought, but this approach should help clear away any confusion around whether the subject of your hex deserves to be locked away or is just a human being who acted unfavorably.

When deciding whether to hex, it can be helpful to ask yourself some basic questions. Did this person hurt you or others? And, if so, did they do so with malicious intent? Did this person continuously harm you or others? And, if so, did they do so with malicious intent? The key here is to define intention and willingness to change, and then you should be able to decide if it is worth hexing that person.

Deciding when to hex has to do with both timing and intention. If you fear that a person or institution is set to oppress or attack another, then you should perform your hex prior to the occasion so as to stop the potential wrongdoing. Hexes can and should be repeated if the person is still in office or a place of authority, or is committing heinous acts. To increase their effect, hexes can be repeated according to the cycles of the moon (see pages 114–115).

Inevitably, there will be times when the call to hex may be unclear. A decision to hex should not be taken lightly, and all possible options should be weighed before you make the final choice. Remember, consider carefully if the act was intentional and whether it was repeated or sustained. The main reason you need to exercise caution here is that the hex may interfere with someone else's free will, which can do far more harm than good. If you feel that this is the case, then just allow the universe to take care of everything on its own. You can always reverse a hex if you need to, but the damage you have potentially created cannot be undone.

DEFENSIVE VS OFFENSIVE MAGIC

The choice between using defensive or offensive magic lies with the severity of the oppression and the ethics of the practitioner. Defensive is meant to protect, while offensive is meant to harm. I choose to work primarily with defensive magic, rather than from a place of vengeance, but even a ward (a type of protective shield or barrier) can have negative effects on the lives of others.

REMEMBER THAT THE FLOW OF ENERGY IS IN THE CONTROL OF THE PRACTITIONER, SO BE WARY OF WHAT YOU ARE GIVING VERUS WHAT YOU ARE RECEIVING.

DEFENSIVE MAGIC:

- Wearing a ward such as a protective amulet (see pages 48–49) or sigil (see pages 46–47) will help to keep the practitioner safe.
- Marking a sigil over a doorway will help to protect an area of practice or rest.
- Binding an oppressor will keep the practitioner from experiencing harm.
- Freezing an oppressor will keep their actions frozen in time.
- Using any form of banishing will create distance between you and your oppressor, but this may just force them out to do more harm to others.
- Healing can be used as a way for an oppressor to come back to their own body, thus encouraging distance.

OFFENSIVE MAGIC:

- Binding spells can also be seen as offensive when the oppressor needs freedom to act out their will.
- Casting a *malocchio* or evil eye (see page 21) will force an oppressor to have bad luck, keeping their attention away from you.
- Working with a poppet (see pages 74–75) can cause pain in your oppressor.
- Using vinegar, lemon, or nails-in-jar spells will sour the environment and create obstacles in life for your oppressor.
- Healing can also be regarded as offensive in the sense that an oppressor may not wish to be healed, and the inevitable psychological issues that they must work through in order to heal may cause a lot of pain.

So, as you can see, the areas of defensive and offensive magic do overlap, but, just like the grayscale, there are always gradients. There will always be consequences when you perform this type of magic, but taking the time to weigh these up should help guide you in deciding whether it is worth performing a hex or not. Please also bear in mind that there may be a possibility for martyrdom in hexing, whether this involves enduring pain to save the masses or sacrificing one to save the collective.
Remember: the choice is always yours and should not be made lightly.

THE
ETHICAL
HEX

Hexing and ethics may seem like apples and oranges, but there is absolutely a way to integrate a stance of integrity when working with darker magic. In fact, it is highly encouraged. In this chapter, you'll learn how to craft your own code of ethics so that you can practice safely.

RULE OF THREE

The number three has long been lauded for possessing an energetic magnetism. You may, for example, have heard someone say: "XYZ always happens in threes" or "Don't do XYZ because it will come back to you, times three."

In numerology, the number three denotes artistry, imagination, and communication. Similarly, in astrology, the Third House (which is ruled by Gemini) is known for its familial relationships, expression, and creativity. The goddesses also come in three forms: maiden, mother, and crone (or the triple goddess). There is clearly something alluring about the number three, as it evokes a feeling of community and creation all rolled into one.

The superstition surrounding the number three can be traced back to the occultist practice of Wicca. The moral system governing Wicca, and indeed many other witchcraft-based faiths, can be summed up by the Wiccan Rede. This hinges around a principle called the Rule of Three, or the Three-Fold Law. This states that whatever energy is sent out into the universe by a person, whether positive or negative, will be returned to that same person three times over. So, taking an example from everyday life, if you were to hurl a hex at someone who bumped into you in the street, you would receive that energy back, times three. Let's say you curse the person in response, wishing that they will get bumped just as you did? Well, you might then find yourself being bumped so hard that you get pushed into the street—only to be hit by a bus.

Sound harsh? It certainly is!

For those that are confused about the difference between Wicca and witchcraft, there is quite a distinction. Wicca is a religion, with rules, regulations, initiations, and ceremonies. Witchcraft, on the other hand, is a customizable practice that leans

"AN' YE HARM NONE, DO WHAT YOU WILL."

more toward an art form, where a person who deems themselves a witch can perform magic in whichever way speaks in the most aligned fashion. There is thus some flexibility in the practice of witchcraft (and hexing), which means not all witches feel that they need to subscribe to the Rule of Three. It is simply a belief system intended to encourage morality and the highest good. It can be helpful to think of the Three-Fold Law in the same way as the punitive intention behind the religious concepts of Heaven and Hell. Christianity has created the idea of two polar resting places in order to illustrate the consequences of not being a "good" human. This is essentially the same as the Three-Fold Law. While some may regard this as a fear-based tactic to get people in line, others may see it as a necessary depiction of the harsh (or blissful) inevitabilities of life.

If you believe in the Three-Fold Law, then you should absolutely adhere to it. If this particular notion doesn't speak to you, however, then you should feel free to cast your own ethical ballot. Ultimately, you need to choose the path that speaks most strongly to you and follow it. The path that enables you to best honor your conscience will be the most successful way forward for you, so keep that in mind as you hex.

THE WICCAN REDE

Bide the Wiccan Law ye must,
In perfect love and perfect trust.
Eight words the Wiccan Rede fulfill:
An' ye harm none, do what ye will.

What ye send forth comes back to thee,
So ever mind the Rule of Three.
Follow this with mind and heart,
Merry ye meet and merry ye part.

ESTABLISHING AN ETHICAL STANCE

The intention behind this section is to help you begin crafting your own ethical stance and set of moral standards. You may find this difficult, but we are not often presented with circumstances that force us into a metaphorical corner and really make us question where our morals lie.

My first job—before teaching you how to hex—is to create a space where you can dig deep enough to understand your own ethical boundaries. These questions and scenarios may be hard to wrap your head around, and you may even find them triggering. So, I urge you to take this section slowly and approach it with care. There is no need to speed through with "yes" or "no" answers if we are aiming to hold the power of someone's life in our hands. I am going to present you with examples using two possible scenarios.

Scenario 1 For the first example, I want you to imagine someone very close to you who you love dearly. And I want you to take a moment and imagine that this person has been hurt very badly by someone you know. What is your gut reaction? Do you want to hurt this person? Do you have an urge for vengeance?

Now, I want you to take a deep breath and imagine that the victim is you. Do you feel slightly differently? How so? Do you feel a possible uptick in anxiety? Or more of a penchant for punishment?

Now, I want you to imagine a stranger as the victim in exactly the same scenario. How does this affect your reaction? Does it somehow become less important?

I have used this example simply to illustrate the emotional and energetic attachment behind vengeance. This energy is incredibly powerful, so it can have marked consequences whenever it is used. The way to decide if a hex is worth casting, is to take yourself out of the equation emotionally, then place yourself fully in it, so that you can view all possible outcomes.

Scenario 2 Imagine now, for this second example, a group of people who are being oppressed and even physically hurt. Does this group have an identity? A specific race? A religion? Does this idea seem far out of reach, or close to home? Do you have a reaction to their mistreatment, or do you decide that it is out of your hands?

Now imagine that this situation is your own, and your own community is being persecuted. What changes for you? How does your ethical and moral stance shift when events have a direct impact on you?

When we speak in terms of political witchcraft, it is interesting to see where we pick our battles. How far are you willing to fight for that which is not your own?

Remember that these questions are merely to make you think about which side of the line you stand on and to encourage you to think outside the box, rather than having emotionally driven, knee-jerk reactions. If you're a lover scorned, for example, be careful not to echo Fúamnach (see page 21) because you are too entrenched in your own drama to see beyond it. And if you are looking to cast a punishment of the highest order, consult your angels first.

EMPOWER YOUR MAGIC

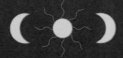

One idea that I like to teach in witchcraft is the power of practical magic. Even the most mundane of tasks can be infused with a little magic, making it more potent and intentional than you might expect.

Many new witches become overwhelmed when approaching the practice of witchcraft because they think that they have to go deep into uncharted woods to find impossible ingredients for spells to work. But the truth is, the power lies within you, and you can channel it into daily tasks in four ways:

By setting boundaries Boundaries are an exceptionally compelling form of magic for a multitude of reasons. When you practice setting boundaries with anyone, you set an energetic tone for how the relationship is to progress. You set a precedence for treatment, and this influences outside perceptions of you. It's an energetic shift that protects you and is essential in all things magical and practical. For example,

refusing to tolerate certain behaviors, and either removing yourself from the situation or putting your foot down to correct the behavior, causes a rift in energy that is recognizable by both parties. You have now created, vibrationally, a barrier between you and mistreatment. Do so by setting the intention for protection against thoughtless actions, or however you would like to specifically tune it, and you have cast a protective spell.

By educating yourself Another form of practical magic lies in educating yourself. If there is one thing that many witches love to do, it is read! So, in terms of politics and magical activism, it is best to do your due diligence and research exactly what it is you are fighting against, rather than throwing hexes blindly into the universe. This strengthens the intention in your actual hex, and you can research magically by setting an intention as well! If you begin your investigation with the intention to "find all the evidence needed to give me a well-rounded view of the subject," you have called upon the universe to guide you in the way of the highest good.

By using words Using your words is a very simple way to cast a spell. For example, if your intention is to change people's perception on a certain topic, you can do so by verbally righting a wrong. If you come across a person with a misguided view of a subject that you can clarify, you can call on your universal guidance to find the courage to speak up and rectify the thought. What you're doing here is invoking a power larger than yourself to act on the highest order. It's quite magical with a reframe!

By engaging politically Finally, voting can be incredibly influential and also quite magical. By doing your research and voting in accordance with your own principles, you can cast a ballot while repeating a mantra or incantation to add some punch to the mix. Saying something to yourself, such as "I call on the universe and the powers that be to carry out the result of the highest good" while in the voting booth can energetically charge your ballot. Remember, intention is absolutely everything when it comes to witchcraft.

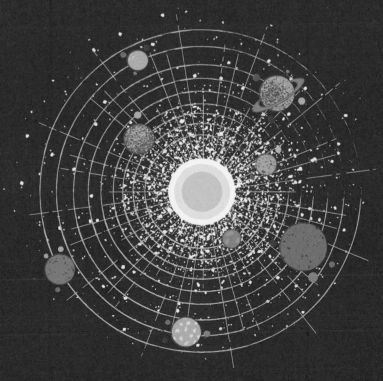

FOCUSING ENERGY

This chapter goes over a witch's most powerful tools: visualization and focused energy. Unless you learn to focus, your magic will not work, so it is essential to practice the lessons in this chapter at length before moving on to spellwork. You can focus energy within yourself using meditative practices, or into an object such as a sigil, amulet, or potion.

MEDITATIVE PRACTICES

Meditation is an excellent way to center yourself and turn your focus to all your personal power. It doesn't have to look like an hour of silence; it is customizable to fit your needs. In the same way as exercise, meditation is a practice that must be worked at consistently. The more you strengthen the meditative muscle, the longer you are able to focus.

Grounding is the first of many ways in which you can meditate. It simply means to secure your energy to the ground. Throughout life, we often go on autopilot or have our head in the clouds, which can bring up feelings of anxiety or a loss of control. Grounding combats this by creating an energetic anchor that brings you back down to the earth, in the present moment. You can practice this method by standing upright, with your eyes closed, and taking a deep breath in and out. When you breathe in, imagine the breath flowing through your lungs and down to the soles of your feet, turning into roots that extend all the way into the earth, securing you to the center. You can repeat this mantra:

**"I AM GROUNDED. I AM SUPPORTED.
I AM ONE WITH THE EARTH."**

Breathing can be an excellent way to focus your energy. This simple act, which keeps us alive and well, is often overlooked and taken for granted, but it is extremely important in both magic and life. In order to breathe intentionally, take one deep breath in and out, in order to center. Then, breathe in for one count, and out for one count. Then, in for two, and out for two, in for three, and out for three, and so on. Continue in this way until you reach 10 (or the highest you can go), then imagine your last breath out in the color red, breathing out passionate, intense, and focused energy. You should instantly feel a shift in your energy.

Body scanning is another way to meditate. I prefer to do this in the bath, but anywhere that you feel comfortable will work. Begin with your eyes closed and, after a few centering breaths, scan—in your imagination while focusing on your body— the very top of your head. Then move down to your forehead, over your eyes, around your ears, your jaw, down your neck, and over your shoulders. You can then move slowly into each arm until you reach the tips of your fingers. Then, return to the chest and scan over the core of your body. And, finally, down each leg into the tips of your toes. Returning focus to each part of your body creates intentional attention to where any pain or tenseness resides, and when you release that tension, your focus becomes sharper.

Maintaining focus during meditation is one of the hardest practices, because we all have wandering thoughts. By observing your thoughts during meditation—like clouds passing in the sky—you can remove your attachment to them and bring your focus back to breath. In this way you actively control your concentration. For this exercise, all you need to do is count your breaths up to the number 10. Every time your mind wanders away from counting, just simply notice and course-correct, right back to counting. This intentionally strengthens the muscle.

Balancing your chakras is a more advanced method of meditating involving visualization. Chakras are energy centers that reside at different points in the body, and we can awaken and balance them by bringing attention to their colored lights. To begin, get into a seated position that is comfortable for you, focus on the top of your head (your crown chakra), and envision a purple light growing from that point. Next, move to the space between your eyes (your third eye chakra) and envision a deeper purple light. Moving next to your throat chakra, and envisioning blue, your heart chakra, glowing green, and then into the space between your ribs. In this area, your solar plexus, you will focus on a yellow light. Then moving to your pelvic bones, your sacral chakra, glowing orange, and the base of your spine, or root, glowing red.

YOU CAN STRENGTHEN THE FOCUS OF THESE ENERGY CENTERS BY REPEATING THESE MANTRAS IN ACCORDANCE WITH EACH CHAKRA:

CROWN *"I receive"*

THIRD EYE *"I open"*

THROAT *"I speak"*

HEART *"I love"*

SOLAR PLEXUS *"I have power"*

SACRAL *"I create"*

ROOT *"I trust"*

THE MIDDLE PILLAR

One of my favorite meditative practices for awakening energy centers before practicing magic is the Middle Pillar exercise. This is a Kabbalistic practice that is similar to the seven chakra centers on the previous page, but instead focuses on five key points in the body.

With this exercise you will repeat Hebraic chants that connect you directly to a higher being (in Hebrew they refer to this being as the Lord), while focusing on growing a corresponding colored light at each point.

Starting at the top of your head, breathe in deeply and focus on a bright white light. With each deep breath, this light will grow brighter. On each exhale, for three exhales, repeat *Eh-Heh-Yeh* ("I am"), feeling the words vibrate in your chest.

Move down to your throat, now breathing in a silver light, growing with each inhale. On the exhales, again three times over, chant *Ye-Hoh-Voh E-Loh-Heem* ("The Lord God").

Moving down the center of the body, illuminate your chest with a gold, glowing light, this time chanting *Ye-Hoh-Voh El-O-Ah-Ve-Da-Ath* ("of Knowledge and Wisdom").

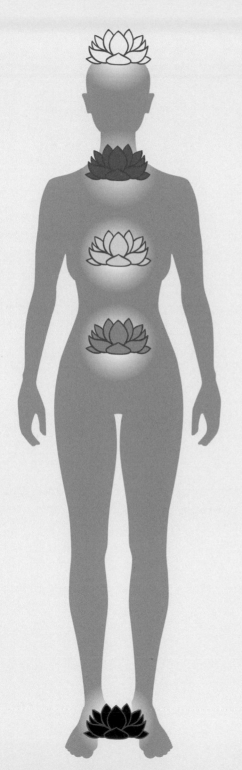

In your belly, the light will glow purple. For this, you repeat *Shah-Dai El Chai* ("The Almighty").

Finally, at your feet, focus on growing a black orb, chanting *Ah-Doh-Nai Ha-Ah-Retz* ("The Lord of the Earth").

Referring to your being as the Lord God might feel entitled at first, but the idea is that we are all one connected being, and you have power over your life and body. Try to keep that in mind if this feels off-putting to you.

I initially practiced this exercise with notes by my side each morning to help me memorize each chant according to the color and energy center. It can be a lot to remember! Don't worry, just practice.

Once you have understood these correspondences, you can commit to learning the flow of energy. To do this, activate each energy center (as described above), then imagine each orb of light flowing like a waterfall down the right side of your body, before flowing back up your left side, all the while using rhythmic breathing. I like to practice this for 10 exhales down the right side and 10 inhales up the left side. You can feel the energy moving through your body, and it's an excellent way to engage with the power within you.

SIGILS

A sigil is a symbol that is crafted by a witch to focus energy on a specific intention. Sigils are very easy to make and have been used by witches for centuries. All you need to make one yourself is a pen and paper.

In medieval witchcraft, ancient occultist grimoires contained sigils (a word meaning *seal* that is derived from Latin). The sigils represented spirits, angels, demons, and the elements. There are 72 sigils for demons in the *Lesser Key of Solomon,* a 17th-century ceremonial magic text, for example. Sigils differ from Norse Runes, which are also symbols, because sigils are created by the practitioner with a base intent, whereas runes are essentially an alphabet with corresponding meanings.

THE TWO MOST IMPORTANT THINGS TO BEAR IN MIND WHEN CRAFTING A SIGIL ARE POSITIVITY AND BREVITY.

So, simply put, a sigil is a symbol that is crafted by the witch with an intention. Sigils can be used for just about anything you can think of. Later, we will learn how to create a sigil for protection (see pages 64-67), just like the witches mentioned earlier.

The two most important things to bear in mind when utilizing a sigil are positivity and brevity. I find that sigils work best within a positive and productive frame of reference, so, instead of using an intention such as "Don't lose money to outside forces," try crafting the intention toward what the practitioner does want—in other words, "Keep money safe from harm." You also need to keep sigil phrases short because repurposing a sigil will be of great use to you. You can record sigils in a notebook, apply them on your face with some foundation (before blending this in), and carve them into your altars. So, instead of using a very long-winded paragraph with confused purpose, keep the intention to a short, focused sentence only. When you learn to create your own sigils later in the book, you will understand how important this brevity is.

CHARGING YOUR SIGIL

Sigils need to be charged by focusing your energy into it so that it works for you. If you practice the meditative tactics described earlier (see pages 40–43), you will be able to do this by channeling the energetic centers in your body into whatever object you desire. Imagine your focused energy flowing into your sigil by concentrating on it and amplifying the power either by rubbing your hands together quickly to create heat and then channeling said heat onto the sigil, or by taking a dab of spit and using this to consecrate your sigil. This might seem a bit off-putting, but witches' spit is believed to be potent and is often used in association with spells!

AMULETS

Amulets are very powerful protective tools that are activated by focusing your energy on them. Many people think that amulets take the form of ancient rubies with Aramaic inscriptions, but they can be just about anything you might wear!

The purpose of an amulet in hexing, and witchcraft in general, is to serve as a protective ward. Witches place an amulet somewhere on their bodies to keep them out of harm's way. To create an amulet, all a witch has to do is consecrate an object by focusing their energy on it.

Choosing your personal amulet should be an intentional act. If you have one in mind that is calling to you for some reason, I recommend following your intuition and using it as your ward. You can choose something to tie on a piece of string to wear around your neck, or even a small trinket to keep in your pocket. Bracelets and earrings work well too—remember, witch*craft* is all about being creative!

When choosing an amulet with the intention of providing protection, perhaps consider a few elements that may help to amplify the protective powers. These include who the previous owner was, as well as its color and design. For example, I have charged a money clip that used to belong to my grandfather as an abundance amulet. As he was the epitome of righteous wealth (in my eyes), and the amulet was literally made for money, I found it to be the perfect fit. Do the same thing for your own amulet: you might want to find something that is black in color to help absorb negativity, or perhaps something symbolic of your chosen deity (see pages 124–125). There are no wrong answers!

CHARGING YOUR AMULET

INSTRUCTIONS

1. You can charge your amulet simply by focusing your energy and intention into it. We have already practiced the basics, but now we are going to channel energy with purpose. In whichever way you see fit, calm your mind and center your energy, grounding firmly into the earth (see pages 40-43). Then, think about your intention and hold it in your mind's eye.

2. Hold your amulet in your hands in front of you and begin to transfer your energy. You can do this by rubbing your hands quickly back and forth across the amulet, creating heat, or simply by envisioning your energy being poured directly into it.

3. Once your amulet is charged with your intention, wear it whenever or wherever you think you'll need protection. You can wear the amulet as often as you like, but, once it breaks, it is thought that the amulet has either served its purpose or broken while protecting you from an outside force. If your amulet breaks, go back to step one and find yourself a new one.

**CHANNEL ENERGY WITH PURPOSE
IN WHICHEVER WAY YOU SEE FIT.**

POTIONS

Potions are excellent ways to "wear" your protection, as you can anoint yourself with a potion anywhere! Plus, this is your chance to stir a concoction in a cauldron and live out your Hocus Pocus–style witch fantasy. Potions are easy to make in the kitchen with very little cleaning up being needed—just be mindful of any allergies you may have.

AS LONG AS YOU FOCUS YOUR ENERGY INTO THE MIXTURE, ITS POWER IS WITH YOU.

Potions can be made by mixing intentional herbs with water. You can also add essential oils, if you wish. Some of my favorite protective herbs are quite easy to find, and you can purchase them either dried or fresh—whatever is available to you. There is a long list of suitable herbs at the back of the book that you can choose from (see pages 120–121), or you can use my favorite herb, basil, if you want to start with something easy.

MAKING YOUR POTION

Add about a cupful of water to a saucepan and bring it to the boil on a stovetop. This is only a small amount of water, so make sure to watch the pan carefully. Next, simply drop in a handful of dried basil and reduce the heat to a simmer. As the herb is energizing the water, stir clockwise and focus your energy into the mixture. Envision a protective energy flowing from your mind and into the pan. You can even whisper an incantation into the water—whatever feels aligned to you, the practitioner. Once the herb is fully saturated, you have a protective potion!

Strain the potion into a bottle and keep it at room temperature. Take care here as some potions may spoil.

You can modify this recipe however you wish, using any herbs you like and also adding essential oils that correspond with your intention. You can also incorporate a cleansing factor using sea salt, if you wish.

USING YOUR POTION

How a potion is used can be different for each witch. For example, you might want to anoint your wrists and pulse points with it, much like a perfume, or spray it about a room to invoke protective energy in the home. You can also spray the potion in your car to help keep you safe on the road. As long as you focus your energy into the mixture, its power is with you.

PROTECTIVE MAGIC

This first spell chapter shows you how to protect yourself with magic before going on the offensive. It is important not to skip this stage, as hexing should only be used as a last resort.

Since we are working with and bending energy, it is very easy for spirits or other energetic sources to join in the fun. Strong feelings exist both for and against your cause. Imagine all these opinions darting randomly through the air like spears, and there you have an idea of chaotic energy.

Creating an energetic protective bubble allows you to focus your intention away from the noise and channel it toward your target. Some witches use a traditional circle to create a safe space to cast their spells. Others prefer different protective methods—I have included a few, so you can choose what works best for you. You can use the spells as stand-alone protection spells, or as a precursor to a more advanced hex. The choice is always yours. On each spell page, I suggest the best time to perform the hex in terms of both the lunar cycle and astrology (see pages 114–117), to maximize its power.

CRYSTAL GRID VISUALIZATION

I invoke protection every morning with a simple meditation that I've constructed using the Kabbalistic Tree of Life as a source of inspiration. Here, I walk you through the energy centers of this concept and teach you how I use it specifically for protection. I prefer to finish my meditation using a Crystal Grid Visualization, but you can modify this last stage to suit your needs.

If you have been practicing the Middle Pillar (see pages 44–45), you will have become used to using Hebrew in ceremonial magic, whether you realize it or not! The Kabbalistic Tree of Life is a very similar concept, just a little more complex. This practice names the energy centers across your body. It differs from the Middle Pillar, which invokes a higher energy while you use them. The Tree of Life also goes through 10 points in your body (see a useful diagram on page 57), rather than the 5 depicted in your center column in the Middle Pillar. So, there are a few more names to get accustomed to in this practice.

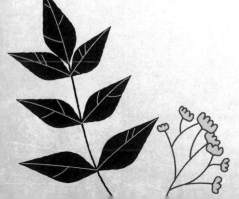

INSTRUCTIONS

1. Starting at the top of your head, much like in the Middle Pillar, focus on growing a white light with each inhale on three passages of breath. This is your crown, or Kether, signifying the integration of divine light with your earthly body.

2. Next, envision the first light connecting to your right temple, your Chokmah, or wisdom source. This is said to be the more masculine part of your brain. Then, move to your left temple, your Binah, or the source of understanding or feminine connection, continuously bridging the light with three inhales per source.

3. Now that your head is fully illuminated and rattling with energy on each inhale, move the light over to your right shoulder. This is your Chesed, or mercy center. This point is said to represent love. Next, move over to your left shoulder, to your Geburah. This light will illuminate the source governing severity or unfiltered judgment. Connect all of these light sources into your gut, or Tiphareth, the source of beauty. This point represents all that makes the self, or the ego.

INSTRUCTIONS CONTINUED

4. From this gut point, connect your light to your right hip, your Netzach of victory. Then, over to the left side, or Zod of splendor, then connect at Yesod, or foundation, which lies in your pelvis or the root of your spine. All three of these points represent higher ascension. Netzach asks your emotions to evolve from petty, base emotions; Zod points to mental magic; and Yesod is the subconscious.

5. Finally, once all nine points are illuminated, send the connecting light fields into your feet, which are your Malkuth or kingdom. This represents the earthly connection of the divine into the material.

6. Practicing illuminating all 10 points takes time, but just remember that diligence will help commit them to memory. You don't have to chant or repeat the names of each energy center as you illuminate them, but it is helpful to know their association as you move through your body.

7. Since this practice is meant to ground and connect you from spirit into earth, I like to use it to protect myself by making the points on my body into a crystal grid each morning. To do this, I stand, then breathe carefully and intentionally through each point I've discussed above. Then, once I feel the connection from the divine to earth, I imagine each point creating something like a crystal cage around my entire body. As I visualize this cage around me, I call out (in my mind) for my spirits to protect me from harm. I sit in this protective grid for a few minutes, and then let it slowly dissolve. If I ever feel unsafe during the day, I just imagine this crystal grid again, and call on its energy to protect me. The more you practice this, the easier it is to invoke!

8. To close your grid, envision the lights you have summoned rematerializing on your body and then shooting up into the universe. This effectively closes your grid on the spiritual plane.

For your own practice, you can use the Kabbalistic Tree of Life method or any that feels most relevant to you. How you construct your protective grid is up to you, but the most important detail is that you feel protected within it. This could mean calling on certain angels, deities, ancestors, prisms, or otherwise. The choice is yours.

TRADITIONAL WITCH'S CIRCLE

To cast a traditional circle for protection, simply spin clockwise, beginning by facing north, with your finger extended outward. Envisioning a white light coming from the tip of this finger, spin three times clockwise while calling Earth, Air, Fire, Water, and Spirit. You are now within your circle and can practice magic within its protection. To close the circle, thank the elements while spinning counterclockwise.

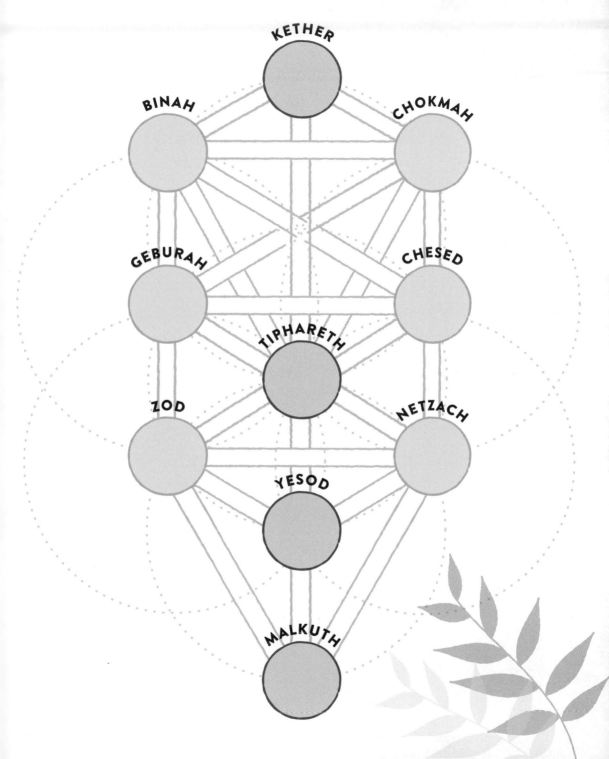

BLACK CANDLE SPELL

This spell is simple to perform, provided you have practiced focusing your energy. The tools and materials are readily available, so there's no need to hunt for rare items. If for some reason you cannot find a black candle, a white one will work just as well. For obvious reasons, please practice fire safety. If you need to extinguish your candle, snuff it out instead of blowing out the flame, as this is said to blow out the intention. However, if you are guided to do so, it is always best to follow your intuition.

YOU WILL NEED

- Basil oil
- Black candle of whatever size you desire
- Lighter or matches

TIMING

This spell is to set an intention for protection, so it is wise to perform it under a new or waxing moon. Fire sign moons are excellent for protection, especially in the case of candle spells.

INSTRUCTIONS

1. Start by casting your protective grid around you and your tools, then begin to ground yourself by noticing how heavy your feet feel rooted into the ground. Work your way up your body, noticing any tightness that may occur. When you feel secure, grab your black candle and basil oil.

2. Coat your palms with two or three drops of oil and focus an intention of protection into the friction as you do so.

3. Take your candle, and from the top and bottom moving inward, coat the candle with the oil, still strongly focusing your energy on the intention of protection.

4. Once your candle is coated and in a safe place for lighting, focus on the wick as you light it and repeat, "I invoke the powers of protection and banishment. Keep me safe from harm." Make sure to practice fire safety.

5. Focus deeply into the flame of the candle and allow yourself to sink into a sort of trance.

6. After a few moments, wake yourself from the meditative state by clapping your hands, then close your grid in whichever way feels good to you.

7. Let the candle burn all the way down, and know that it is done.

BLACK SALT SCRUB

This spell is also a great beauty DIY! While it is hyper-exfoliating and nourishing for your skin, this scrub is also a potent defense against gossip and slander. For this spell, I like to think of the phrase "I am rubber, you are glue." The scrub acts as a defense mechanism. Just make sure to have no open wounds on your body, as the salt will irritate them. Keep the scrub in the refrigerator after hexing. This stops the lemon from spoiling, which creates a sour energy over your protection ward.

YOU WILL NEED
- ¼ cup black sea salt
- ½ fresh lemon
- 1 tbsp coconut oil
- Mixing bowl and spoon

TIMING

This spell is great for banishment, so it is wise to perform it under a dark moon. This is the last phase of the waning moon.

INSTRUCTIONS

1. Begin by grounding in your preferred way with all of your ingredients at hand.

2. First, toss the black sea salt into the mixing bowl. Black salt is excellent for cleansing, banishment, and protection.

3. Next, squeeze the lemon into the bowl. Lemon is known to purify.

4. Finally, add the coconut oil to the bowl. Coconut is moon-ruled, so will help to call upon the energies of the subconscious.

5. With all of your ingredients before you, start stirring them together in a counterclockwise direction to make the body scrub. As you stir, whisper the words: "banish negative energies" three times into the bowl.

6. Now that your scrub is made and consecrated with your intention, it's time to shower!

7. While you are in the shower, cast your chosen protective grid around you before you begin.

8. Take the scrub and rub it over your body in a counterclockwise direction. As you rub, imagine all the negative speech that has been thrown your way is dissipating directly off your skin.

9. Wash off the mixture and imagine the hateful speech swirling down the drain, flowing away completely.

10. Continue showering as usual, and close off your grid in the way that you see fit.

OBSIDIAN AMULET

Using obsidian in your amulet amplifies the protective aspect by adding in the healing powers of this ancient stone. It may be difficult to source your perfect amulet, but keep your eyes peeled for the right one that calls to you. To help, you could set an intention to find a piece of obsidian that will best protect you, and call in the manifestation of said object. When it appears in your life, you will know it was sent to protect you. This will make your amulet even more powerful, as you were guided to it by the universe.

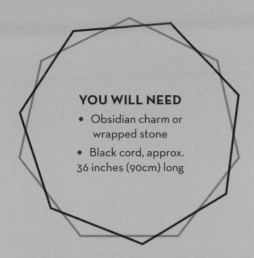

YOU WILL NEED

- Obsidian charm or wrapped stone
- Black cord, approx. 36 inches (90cm) long

TIMING

This spell is great for setting the intention for protection, so new and waxing moons are ideal. However, you should wear your amulet at all times.

INSTRUCTIONS

1. Begin by casting your protective grid around you and your tools, and begin to ground.

2. Take your perfect piece of obsidian in your hands and focus your energy directly into it.

3. As you are holding the obsidian, imagine the divine energy of your protective grid being poured directly into the stone, soaking up its innate ability to protect you from harm.

4. Once your intuition suggests that you have poured in sufficient energy, lace the black cord through the stone to make a necklace.

5. Tie the amulet around your neck, knotting it three times behind your back, to signify the triple goddess.

6. Once the amulet is firmly in place, sit and let the obsidian stone connect to your heart's center.

7. After a few moments, close your grid in whichever way feels good to you. Keep the amulet around your neck whenever you are in need of protection (you can wear it when you sleep and shower, but this is not necessary). If it breaks, you know the amulet has served its purpose and you can repeat the spell.

SIGILS FOR PROTECTION

Throughout history, witches have used magically charged symbols called sigils to hold a specific intention and protect, heal, and manifest. They are quite easy to create, but are extremely powerful.

THE CREATION

Sigils are created by writing out an intention, and then using a sequence of letters to make them into an appealing shape. Depending on your style, you can choose whatever artistic direction you'd like when creating your sigil. The steps are generally the same, but you can either use a witch's wheel to help guide when arranging your letters or arrange them however you'd like. The most important aspects of a sigil, however, are that it contains your intention, resonates with you, and is charged to hold your magic (see page 47). Once it is created and charged, you can write this magical symbol on whichever and however many surfaces you desire to bring in that magic. You can carve a sigil on candles, draw it in your grimoire, or even anoint your skin with makeup or oil in the sigil design before it is absorbed into your skin.

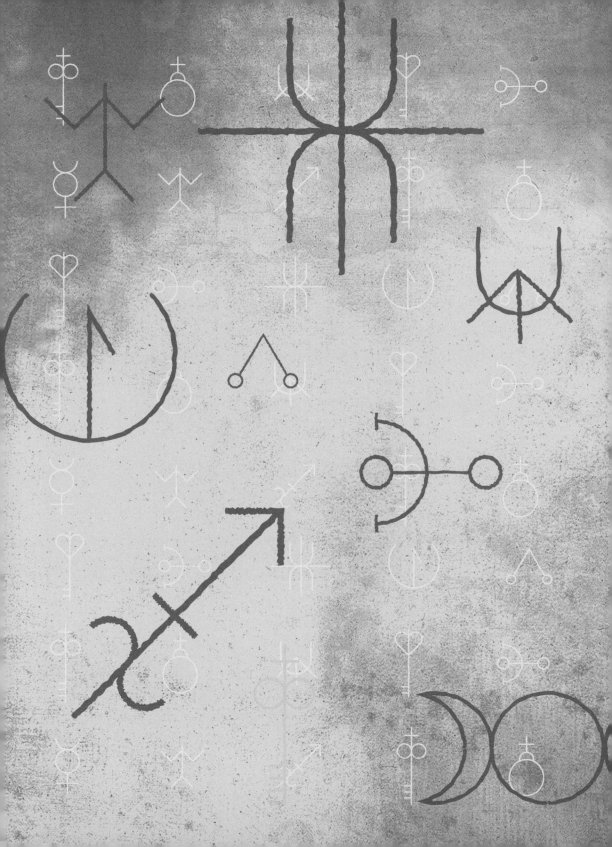

INSTRUCTIONS

1. Writing your intention

For the purpose of protection, it is important to be specific when writing an intention. For example, "Keep me and my fellow citizens safe from harm" can be misconstrued, because harm to one can be protection to another. Something more specific could be: "Keep me and my neighbors safe from white supremacists." Now we have a direction for the universe.

2. Finding your letters

Once you have your intention—in this case "Keep me and my neighbors safe from white supremacists"—you can now cross out all vowels that appear in the statement. You will be left with these letters:

KPMNDMNGHBRSSF
FRMWHTSPRMCSTS

3. Whittling it down

From here, cross out all the repeating letters. You will then be left with this:

KPMNDGHBRSFWTC

These are the letters you will use to make your sigil.

4. The design

Beginners should use a witch's wheel to arrange their letters (see opposite). You simply mark points on the wheel for each letter and connect the dots. Once your wheel is finished, you are ready to charge and consecrate (see page 47). You can then place this sigil in your neighborhood to keep your community safe.

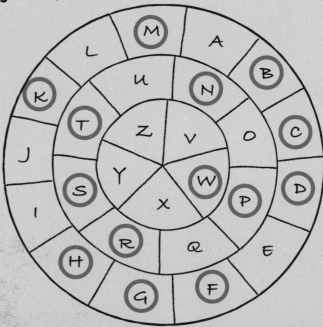

THE **WITCH'S WHEEL**

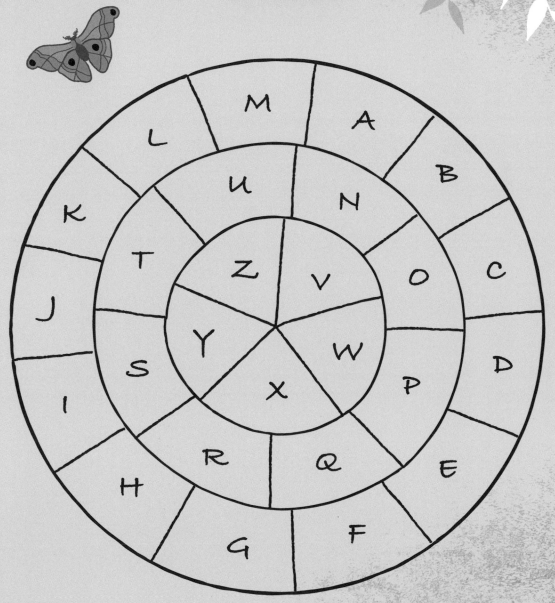

BINDING AND FREEZING SPELLS

Binding and freezing spells mark a step up from protective spells. These types of spells will stop a harasser in their tracks and keep them from committing more harm. So, before escalating to this next stage, check first whether your baseline protective spells might be enough to keep the person or entity at bay.

Please be aware that binding and freezing will keep the object of your hex stuck, which could lead to unexpected consequences. Take, for example, a judge on the Supreme Court. If a track record indicates that they have overwhelmingly voted in favor of the patriarchy, then you may feel inclined to hex. However, if you do, and the judge becomes the deciding vote on a bill that must be passed—and you have hindered their ability to choose a side—there could be intense ramifications.

So, before going ahead, always think clearly and thoroughly about who and what you're hexing, and even more, why you're hexing. You should certainly be well equipped to handle the consequences of what you've cast out.

BLACK CORD RITUAL

This spell is excellent for binding hate groups to prevent them from causing harm, and it is particularly useful when challenging the patriarchy. Since hate groups contain more than one person, this type of ritual is especially powerful when done with a coven, as a solo practitioner will find that their powerful energy meets a lot of resistance. It is said that conflicting views will be at war on another plane, so in order to amplify the power of what is just, create a group to practice with.

YOU WILL NEED:

- Photograph of the subject of your hex
- Black cord, approx. 36 inches (90cm) long
- Glass jar with a lid

TIMING

This spell can be done under the energy of the dark moon, or you can use the new moon to set out your intention to bind or freeze. Harnessing the energy of the full moon could also work well with the climax of light, as you are expelling out hateful acts. Choosing which moon feels aligned will be up to the practitioner. Using signs like Aries or Scorpio, which are ruled by Mars, the warrior planet, will help to carry your intention.

1. Cast your protective grid around you and your tools, and begin to ground. If you are practicing with others, make sure to all invoke your grids or cast a protective circle around everyone involved in the group.

2. Ground by connecting with the floor beneath you, while either standing or sitting, whichever is more comfortable, and holding your tools. If you are in a coven, everyone should hold their own tools.

3. State your intention to bind the figure in your photograph. This might be a hate group or a member of the patriarchy. As long as you have a photographic representation of your intended hexing target, you will be able to cast effectively.

4. Once you have stated your intention, take the photograph in your non-dominant hand (to represent release) and the black cord in your dominant hand (to represent control).

5. Begin wrapping the cord around the photograph in a clockwise direction to call in the bind.

6. As you are wrapping, state, "I bind ____ from doing harm against ____." It is very important to be specific with this intention, so don't cast too broad a hex.

7. Continue wrapping your photograph until it is completely covered. Then place the wrapped photograph in the jar and put on the lid. At this point, you can close your circle if you've cast one.

8. Either bury the jar to initiate permanence or keep it in a safe corner in your home, surrounded by rosemary to contain the energy.

STOP THE GOSSIP

This spell keeps slander from escaping the mouth of your subject. You will be binding them to stay quiet with energetic force. It is best to use this spell when dealing with a dictatorship and hate speech, rather than if someone simply said something you don't like.

If you can rectify the behavior with a simple conversation, chances are it's not worthy of a hex. However, I trust that by reading this book, you have begun to craft your own moral code, and will know when to cast and when not to. Just remember that if you do keep someone from speaking, they can also be stopped from saying what is good and/or needed.

YOU WILL NEED:

- Photograph of the subject of your hex
- Piece of tape
- Safe space to bury or keep

TIMING

This spell is designed to banish toxic speech, so use it during a waning moon phase. Fire sign moons and Scorpio are great for this type of work; however, Air signs govern communication and can work just as well. Aquarius in particular governs social change.

4. Take the photograph of your subject, and the tape.

5. With the photograph and tape in your hand, say out loud, "I keep ___ from doing harm by speaking. I call on the forces of good to keep the universe in balance by keeping ___ quiet."

6. Focus deeply on the photograph, then place a piece of tape to cover the subject's mouth.

7. Use your hands to channel all your energy into your intention. You may also do this in a group, with everyone channeling their energy into one photograph.

8. Once you have focused sufficiently (you will know by your intuition), remove your hands and shake them out.

9. Bury the photograph, still with the tape attached, in the earth or keep it hidden in a drawer or closet. It is done.

INSTRUCTIONS

1. Begin by casting your protective grid around you and your tools, then begin to center yourself.

2. Breathe deeply through your lips and focus on your inward breath, creating an intentional space where you control what you consume. Breathe out through your pursed lips and create an intentional space where you control what you expel. Repeat this until you feel calm.

3. Next, focus on your throat chakra and begin to balance it. You can do this by imagining a soft blue light glowing in your throat with each inhale.

PATRIARCHAL POPPET

Poppets have been used for centuries to perform acts of folk magic, in both healing and hexing. The most popularized version of a poppet is the voodoo doll in African and Caribbean cultures.

However, the term *poppet* has essentially been used in European cultures to define the same thing. Poppets are usually made out of corn husks or other items in the hearth. In this spell, you will be creating a likeness of your subject and using it to hex or heal. If you don't feel creative enough to do this, then simply take a doll and adorn it with your subject's personal possessions (clothing, hair, skin, fingernails). This might be impossible for obvious reasons (if your subject is not someone you know, for example), but I will give you the basics here.

YOU WILL NEED:

- Photograph of your subject
- Black sock
- Stuffing (found at a craft store)
- Piece of black tourmaline
- Needle and black thread

TIMING

This spell can be performed under any moon phase, provided it matches your intention. If you are setting the intention to bring healing to your subject, a new or waxing moon is ideal. If you are looking to banish harm, a waning or dark moon will fit best. A full moon can combine both intentions. However, performing under a moon in an Earth sign will help to bring your intention into the body.

INSTRUCTIONS

1. Begin by grounding in your preferred way with all of your tools before you.

2. Take a moment to bless your space. Make sure to begin with a clean and pure energy, then state your intention out loud.

3. Next, hold the photograph of your subject in your hands. Focus your intention into it. Fold it one time toward you, then set it aside.

4. Begin to fill the sock with the stuffing. As you fill the sock, imagine life being poured into it. Imagine adding meat to the inside of a body.

5. Now, place the photograph inside the middle of the sock. Imagine you are placing a heart in your poppet.

6. Then, blow into your poppet, imagining that you are breathing life into it.

7. Place the black tourmaline next to the photograph of your subject. Black tourmaline is meant to transform energy positively. This will send the transformation to the heart of your subject.

8. Finally, use the needle and thread to sew up the bottom of the sock. With each stitch, repeat your intention.

9. Keep your poppet in a safe space, in a closet or a drawer, where it can be kept untouched. It is done.

FREEZING THE MAN

Freezing spells are a hexing go-to for many witches. These types of spells effectively "freeze" the subject in their tracks. I will add a warning here, however, because if a person is effectively frozen, they will be kept from performing any task the universe associates with your intention. In all these spells—and this bears repeating—remember to look at the full 360-degree view before blindly throwing out hexes.

YOU WILL NEED:

- Photograph of your subject
- Glass jar with a lid
- Filtered water or water of your choice (thunderstorm, snow, ocean, river)
- Freezer

TIMING

This simple spell is inherently for banishing behavior, so it fits best with waning and dark moons. Since water is used, Water moons are appropriate, but be sure you have a handle on your emotions before proceeding and ground correctly.

INSTRUCTIONS

1. Cast your protective grid around you and your tools, then begin to connect with the earth beneath your feet.

2. Once you feel secure in your body, take the photograph of your subject and focus your intention of freezing directly into it.

3. Place the photograph in the jar.

4. Now add your choice of water to the jar. Don't fill the jar up all the way, as water expands when it freezes, but add just enough water to cover the photograph. If you use filtered water, you will have a pure vessel for your intention. You can also use other types of water—water from a thunderstorm to carry swift force, melted water from snow to amplify the freezing power, ocean water to add the protection and sting of salt, and river water to carry your intention with a certain flow.

5. Water provides a clear channel to speak to spirits—whisper your intention into the jar before you put on the lid.

6. Once your jar is sealed tight, place it at the back of your freezer and keep it there for as long as you believe it is needed.

7. When you remove the jar and empty out the contents, the hex will be broken. Discard the photograph and water outside to rid your home of any hexed items.

BIND RUNES

Runes are ancient alphabets that carry an intention with each character. The first runic alphabet can be dated back to AD 800, but the most commonly known runes are those of the Celtic and Nordic alphabets. These symbols have secret, magical meanings, and when woven together to create a bind, they can be very powerful. In this spell, you will be constructing a bind using these characters to fit your exact intention. I will give you the basics to construct your own.

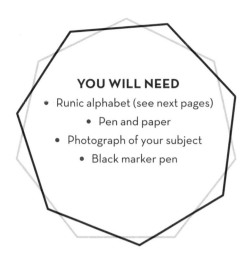

YOU WILL NEED

- Runic alphabet (see next pages)
- Pen and paper
- Photograph of your subject
- Black marker pen

TIMING

This spell intends to bind, so I find a new and waxing moon to bring in the bind to be the most appropriate. Since runes are generally made from earth, and we want to constrict the body, Earth moons fit best.

INSTRUCTIONS

1. Cast your protective grid around you and your tools, then begin to ground.

2. Once centered, write your intention on a piece of paper and begin to pick runes from the alphabet on the following pages that match with your intention. For example, if you are looking to freeze or bind, use the runes for "freeze," "defense," and "warrior."

3. Next, you will draft your bind rune underneath your intention. There are different ways to combine your runes. If you connect them in a linear pattern, following one line in a vertical fashion, you will be mimicking what warriors used on their weapons. If you combine the runes in a radial fashion, connecting them at a central point almost like a pinwheel, you are channeling an ancient defense spell.

Finally, you can combine your runes in a more puzzle-piece fashion, called multi-axel, which will help with manifestation. For multi-axel, you choose a central rune and build off it.

4. Once you have designed your bind rune in the way that you see fit, take your draft as a template and then draw it on top of your subject's photograph with the black marker pen.

5. As you are drawing, focus your intention into the bind rune. Connect with that energy and pour it in.

6. Once it is sufficiently charged, take the photograph and place it somewhere where it will be kept undisturbed, such as in a drawer or closet. It is done.

THE RUNIC ALPHABET

FEHU (cattle)
Earthly meaning: success ~ abundance ~ earned wealth ~ good fortune
Spiritual meaning: fulfillment ~ growth ~ expansion

URUZ (wild ox)
Earthly meaning: strength ~ courage ~ determination ~ opportunity
Spiritual meaning: initiation ~ life change ~ meeting one's destiny

THURISAZ (thorn)
Earthly meaning: protection ~ barriers ~ pride ~ self-deception
Spiritual meaning: destruction and rebirth ~ inner truth ~ false ego

ANSUZ (wisdom)
Earthly meaning: learning ~ communication ~ contemplation ~ wise counsel
Spiritual meaning: divine aid ~ creative spark ~ initiation

RAIDO (wagon)
Earthly meaning: travel ~ communication ~ decisive action ~ reunion
Spiritual meaning: inner path ~ destiny

KENAZ (torch)
Earthly meaning: knowledge ~ new outlook ~ understanding ~ ideas
Spiritual meaning: inner guidance ~ enlightenment

GEBO (gift)
Earthly meaning: success ~ union ~ happiness ~ obligation
Spiritual meaning: karma ~ inner equilibrium

WUNJO (joy)
Earthly meaning: happiness ~ celebration ~ harmony ~ family
Spiritual meaning: inner peace ~ at one with the universe

HAGALAZ (hai)
Earthly meaning: destruction ~ damage ~ distress ~ disruption
Spiritual meaning: inner crisis ~ doubt ~ transformation

NAUDHIZ (need)
Earthly meaning: needs ~ self-restraint ~ avoidance of greed ~ patience
Spiritual meaning: asceticism ~ transcendence ~ the soul

ISA (ice)
Earthly meaning: obstacles ~ standstill ~ caution ~ patience
Spiritual meaning: inner calm ~ surrender ~ introspection

JERA (harvest)
Earthly meaning: reward ~ fruition ~ maturity ~ growth
Spiritual meaning: right action ~ natural law

EIHWAZ (yew)
Earthly meaning: problem-solving ~ strength under attack ~ protection
Spiritual meaning: resurrection ~ transcendence

PERTHO (secret)
Earthly meaning: chance ~ gambling ~ secrets ~ windfall ~ birth
Spiritual meaning: fate ~ the feminine

ᛉ ALGIZ (protection)
Earthly meaning:
protection ~ assistance ~
advancement ~ persistence
Spiritual meaning:
guardian spirit ~ divine
intervention ~ mysticism

ᛋ SOWILU (sun)
Earthly meaning: vitality ~
good health ~ good fortune
~ happiness
Spiritual meaning: blessing
~ wholeness

ᛏ TEIWAZ (authority)
Earthly meaning: justice ~
passion ~ drive ~ victory
Spiritual meaning: the
greater good ~
righteousness

ᛒ BERKANA (birch)
Earthly meaning: creativity
~ new ideas ~ birth ~
nourishment
Spiritual meaning: mother
energy ~ inner growth

ᛖ EHWAZ (horse)
Earthly meaning: moving ~
progress ~ travel ~
cooperation ~ partnership
Spiritual meaning: inner
progress ~ duality of nature

ᛗ MANNAZ (man)
Earthly meaning: family ~
friendship ~ charitable
deeds ~ the greater good
Spiritual meaning: the self
~ transcendence ~
communion

ᛚ LAGUZ (water)
Earthly meaning: journey
across water ~ intuition ~
fluidity ~ creativity
Spiritual meaning:
premonitions ~
unconscious desires ~ the
unknown

ᛜ INGWAZ (potency)
Earthly meaning:
achievement ~ difficulties
overcome ~ creativity ~
fertility
Spiritual meaning: unity ~
equanimity

ᛟ OTHILA (home)
Earthly meaning:
inheritance ~ property ~
family ~ responsibilities
Spiritual meaning:
universal truths

ᛞ DAGAZ (day)
Earthly meaning: hope ~
relief ~ clarity ~
understanding ~ progress
Spiritual meaning: destiny
~ higher consciousness ~
mutability

ᚹ WYRD (fate)
Earthly meaning:
uncertainty ~ unknown
consequences ~
acceptance
Spiritual meaning: the
unknowable ~ fate

BANISHING SPELLS

This spell chapter is perfect for getting rid of unwanted energy. When you need to remove someone from your space, these are the spells to choose. In terms of the patriarchy, you can banish those that have dominion over your rights or those that are exercising power over a disenfranchised group. With these spells under your belt, you will be better equipped to protect those that need it.

Some of my favorite banishing spells operate simply by saying "No." Banishment is a great way to set both physical and energetic boundaries. You are exerting an actual barrier between you and your subject, whether this is verbal, tangible, or magical. I would suggest, in terms of banishment, to use courage first. If you can bravely and safely tell your target to go away, I would start there. Banishment spells are ideal for targets that are not easily accessed by the practitioner who then has to find other means of excommunicating the aggressor.

VINEGAR SOUR JAR

This spell puts a little sting into banishment, so be very careful with it. As with every spell in this book, I caution you to use your ethical code to determine if your subject is fully deserving.

With this spell, you will not only banish the subject to a space where they are unable to harm, you will also cause misfortune in their new space. This is a harsh treatment, but it also creates the notion that, even in a new arena, your subject will be unable to cause pain and suffering to others.

YOU WILL NEED:

- Photograph of your subject
- Glass jar
- Filtered water or water of your choice (thunderstorm, snow, ocean, river)
- White vinegar
- Park or outdoor space away from your home

TIMING

This spell is best performed under a waning moon, as you are releasing and expelling energy. For a quick effect, use Fire moons. For permanence, use Earth moons.

INSTRUCTIONS

1. Begin by casting your protective grid around you and your tools, then start to ground and anchor into the earth.

2. Once you are grounded, take your tools and state your intention. The phrasing should be similar to: "Spirits, please guide me in banishing ___" but use whatever phrasing feels aligned to your practice.

3. Holding your photograph, focus your energy onto your subject. As you are concentrating, imagine your subject turning away and leaving, moving through a door that shuts behind them. Hold this vision in your mind's eye.

4. Next, half fill the jar with your choice of water. You may use thunderstorm water to create a dramatic exit, river water to "push" the subject out, ocean water to add cleansing, or simply filtered water to act as a conduit.

5. Take your vinegar and fill your jar the rest of the way. As you pour, imagine your subject being too distraught to focus on anything else but their own circumstances. Keep this visualization strong.

6. Once your jar is full, put the lid on tightly and state your intention, again out loud.

7. You may close your grid whenever you feel aligned. As soon as possible, take your jar to a space away from your home, preferably a park or wooded area. Leave your jar where it will be untouched, and you have successfully banished your target.

BANISHING AMULET

This amulet is perfect for repelling violence. If you are personally experiencing harassment, wearing this amulet will help to banish that energy. It should be noted, however, that this is not a substitute for contacting the authorities. Instead, it is supplemental to purify the toxicity of the environment.

If you are not experiencing any type of violence, but instead know of a place where violence occurs, this amulet will radiate a cleansing energy to that particular spot. For this amulet, I suggest using the stone garnet, which purifies and balances energy. It also has very passionate properties, which makes it perfect for banishment. However, if you feel drawn to something else with the same intention, please use that.

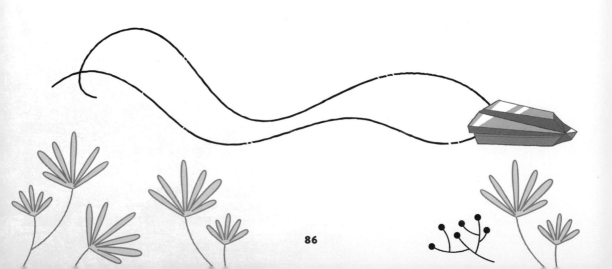

YOU WILL NEED

- Garnet charm or wrapped stone
- Black cord, approx. 36 inches (90cm) long (optional)

TIMING

Since this amulet is meant to banish, you should perform the spell itself on a waning moon. However, the amulet will continuously carry this banishing energy until it breaks. Using Scorpio or Aries moons will be most effective, as both signs are ruled by the warrior planet, Mars.

INSTRUCTIONS

1. Begin by casting your protective grid around you and your tools, and begin to ground and anchor to the earth.

2. Once you have your perfect piece of garnet, take it in your hands and focus your energy directly into it.

3. As you are holding the garnet, imagine the banishment of all forms of violence being poured directly into the charm, soaking up its ability to expel toxicity. For this particular visualization, I recommend calling on a warrior goddess, such as Kali, to help bring the energy of banishment.

4. After your intuition indicates that you have poured in sufficient energy, lace the black cord through the charm, making it into a necklace if you so prefer. If your amulet is to be worn in your pocket, or tucked away in a particular place, you may skip this step.

5. Once the charm is threaded onto the cord, tie it around your neck, knotting it three times behind your back, signifying the triple goddess.

6. Once your amulet is firmly in place, sit and let it connect to your heart's center.

7. After a few moments close your grid in whichever way feels good to you.

8. Keep your amulet around your neck at all times that you are in need of this banishing energy (you can wear it when you sleep and shower, but this is not necessary). If it breaks, you know the amulet has served its purpose and you can repeat the spell. Similarly, if you are placing your amulet somewhere, keep it in a spot that is unseen, and it will banish violence.

BANISHING POWDER

This spell was inspired by the use of Hot Foot Powder, a common spell in hoodoo. Hot Foot Powder is used to drive unwanted people away, being sprinkled on clothing or in shoes. It could drive out a range of negative energies, from pesky to abusive.

For this particular spell, you'll be using these same principles, but instead of sprinkling the powder directly on your target (assuming you do not have direct contact with the subject of the patriarchy you have deemed important), you will be using a photograph.

Another common tool in rootwork, hoodoo, and folk magic is the use of a crossroads. It is said that you can petition the spirits to help carry your intention at this point. It could be an intersection near your home, but make sure you can perform this spell uninterrupted and safely.

As this spell comes from disenfranchised groups that have been consistently beaten down by the patriarchy, I suggest using it to drive out white supremacy. Keep this in mind when choosing your target.

YOU WILL NEED

- 1 tbsp dried chili flakes
- 1 tbsp cayenne pepper
- 1 tbsp table salt
- 1 tbsp black pepper
- 1 tbsp dried oregano
- Mixing bowl
- Photograph of your subject
- Crossroads

TIMING

This spell is great for banishment, so it is wise to perform it under a waning or dark moon. I find that Fire moons are best for banishment, but Earth moons can also work well to influence permanence.

INSTRUCTIONS

1. Begin by grounding in your preferred way with all of your ingredients at hand.

2. First, take the mixing bowl and begin to add your ingredients.

3. When all the ingredients are added, mix them together with your hand, channeling your intention directly into them. As you mix, state your intention either out loud, or in your head, focusing on the mixture.

4. Once everything is sufficiently mixed, take your photograph and mixing bowl and head out to a crossroads.

5. Place the photograph of your subject on the ground at the crossroads. This should not be in the center, where you could get injured, but at a corner instead.

You can even use the southernmost corner, which is associated with Fire, to put an extra burn on your banishment.

6. With the photograph of your subject on the ground, begin pouring the mixture over the photograph. As you are dousing your subject, state your intention again. Make sure the photograph is sufficiently covered.

7. When you have finished covering the photograph, say a quick "Thank you" to the spirits of the crossroads who will help to carry your intention to fruition.

8. Leave the photograph in place. If you have any mixture left, make sure to dispose of it outside your home.

BANISHING CANDLE

For this spell you are going to be using both fire and a sigil to cast out sexism. Fire has a quick and passionate return, and sigils have been used to protect and call in fertility for centuries, which are both intentions traditionally associated with female archetypes. If you need help creating a sigil, see pages 64–67 for detailed instructions.

If you have a direct experience of sexism, you may use this spell to banish your connection. If you are looking to perform this spell for collective well-being, performing it with the extra energy of a coven would be appropriate.

YOU WILL NEED:

- Pen and paper
- Black candle
- Dowel or other carving tool
- Lighter or matches

TIMING:

Again, this spell is for banishment, so performing it during a waning or dark moon is most appropriate. Fire moons are great for banishment, and great to use with candle spells. However, since this particular intention has to do with the divine feminine, Water and Earth moons are also quite powerful.

INSTRUCTIONS

1. Begin by casting your protective grid around you and your tools, then begin to ground.

2. Take the pen and paper and write out your intention. This can be personal or universal.

3. Once you have written down your intention, create your sigil.

4. When the draft of your sigil is finished, take the black candle and dowel. Begin to carve your sigil into your candle, focusing your intention with each stroke of the dowel as you carve.

5. Once you have carved your sigil, take a dab of your own spit and anoint the candle with it. If you are in a coven, have everyone do this step.

6. Finally, light the anointed candle, focusing on the flame with your intention held strong. When you feel that you have channeled sufficient energy, bring yourself back to your surroundings by clapping once in front of your face. You may also release your grid. Make sure to practice fire safety.

7. Let the candle burn all the way down, but make sure it stays in a safe space as it does so. You may snuff out the flame if necessary, just be mindful not to blow it out.

EXORCISING INTERNALIZED OPPRESSION

This spell is intended to deprogram our thoughts. While growing up "in the system," we adopt feelings and biases that are not our own. As a result, we begin to collect evidence to support these thoughts and, over time, the consequences can be dire.

Disenfranchised groups are constantly victims of these internalized thoughts, whether we are conscious of them or not. In fact, the less aware we are of our programming, the more dangerous it becomes. This spell uses the principles of shadow work to bring up our deepest biases, and by illuminating them, we can effectively banish them.

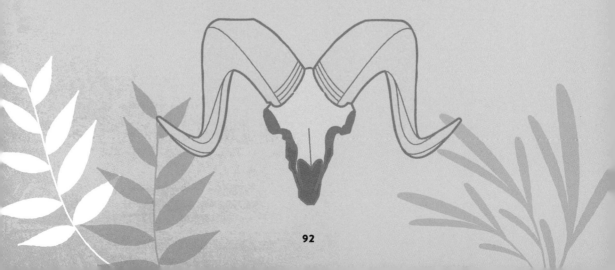

YOU WILL NEED:

- Pen and paper

TIMING:

This spell is excellent to do under waning and dark moons and is especially potent under Water moons. Because Water moons have the ability to access your deepest emotions, this spell can be cast quite powerfully.

INSTRUCTIONS

1. Cast your protective grid around you and your pen and paper, then begin to ground and anchor into the earth.

2. Once you are comfortable and feel secure, take the pen and paper, then write down the following prompts:

What is your earliest memory around skin color? What emotional attachments do you have around this memory?

Have you ever held a bias against someone because of their skin color, whether this was positive or negative?

What is your earliest memory regarding gender?

What assumptions do you hold about different gender expressions and gender identities?

What is your earliest memory regarding sexual orientation? Does this influence any biases?

How do you respond to a gender, sexual orientation, or skin color other than your own in a position of power and authority?

Has anyone "different" from you ever made you feel uneasy? How so, and why?

3. Use these prompts to dig deep and be honest with yourself. There is no need to hold on to any shame surrounding your answers. Instead, continue to ask yourself "Why?" until you get to the root.

4. Once you have sufficiently noted down these biases, take the piece of paper and rip it into shreds, stating "I denounce these biases, and banish the notion that I treat anyone differently based on gender, race, or sexual orientation."

5. Take the scraps of paper and toss them in a trash can outside. Remember your findings, and then commit to making small changes each day.

HEALING SPELLS

As we saw earlier in the book: if you can't hex, you can't heal. This chapter aims to take the high road by healing your aggressors if the climate allows for such patience and acts of kindness. With focused energy and the desire to heal deep wounds, the energy of the patriarchy, for example, can be softened and eased.

Many people commit hateful acts as a way of projecting their own hurt. Instead of addressing biases, trauma, and pain, they hurt others to lessen these issues. But this only passes the cycle of trauma on to new victims. Healing the root of the pain wielded by the patriarchy like a sword can usher in a new wave of understanding that does more than just put a Band-Aid on oppression, but hopefully eliminates it, too.

This chapter also makes us take a closer look at ourselves. Why are we so quick to hex? Is it the most viable option, or are we merely projecting our own pain? Healing is a universal tool that we all need and should consistently work toward.

HEALING CANDLE

This spell wishes healing on the men and male-identifying people of the nation. By focusing your energy on this candle, you are aiming to heal any wounds created by toxic masculinity.

When children are born, they are untouched by the stigmas of our culture, yet as they grow up, they become targets of unnecessary aggression and are held to an ignorant idea of what masculinity really is. While this is not an excuse for anyone who harbors and repeats the ideals of toxic masculinity, this spell aims to heal those who are too blind to see that they are stuck in the cycle.

YOU WILL NEED
- Pink candle
- Lighter or matches
- Dowel or other carving tool

TIMING
This spell is best performed under a new or waxing moon, as you are wishing to bring something in. Since this is a candle spell, it is very appropriate to use Fire moons. However, you may also use emotional Water moons or grounded Earth moons.

INSTRUCTIONS

1. Start by casting your protective grid around you and your tools, then begin to ground and anchor into the earth.

2. Once you are grounded, take your tools and state your intention out loud. Your intention can be for universal healing, or you can direct it toward a specific subject. The choice is yours. I quite like the intention: "I desire to influence men afflicted with toxic masculinity to experience the divine feminine and know its power."

3. Use the dowel to carve a symbol into the side of the candle. You may carve a healing sigil, the name of your subject, or simply a heart. However you feel called to express the divine feminine.

4. Next, light the candle and focus intensely on the flame, and then imagine a glowing, soft pink light emanating from it. Make sure to practice fire safety.

5. As you watch the pink glow, work on expanding it. Visualize this glow growing. If you can do this with your eyes open, excellent. If not, simply close your eyes or soften your gaze, and visualize this glow growing so large that it fills the room, then expands outside your home.

6. Keep growing the pink glow until it envelopes the world, starting with the initial flame and expanding into the universe.

7. Once you have expanded the glow, hold it in your mind's eye for a few moments, and then imagine it slowly dissolving across the globe, filtering and falling into the hearts of those who need it.

8. It is done. Snuff out the candle. Do not blow it out, as this can also blow out your intention. Close your grid whenever you feel aligned.

OPEN EYES SPELL

This spell helps open ignorant eyes to the beauty and diversity of the world. In a deeply meditative state, you will focus on lifting the fog of hate that so often comes with a clear incomprehension of the struggles of others.

There are many different ways you can use this spell; you can cast it on the collective, on a particular subject, or even on yourself. If you are having a difficult time seeing another's viewpoint, then this spell can be quite enlightening.

I've also found that this spell works especially well on family members or employers who can't see where you're coming from. By wishing a healing and illuminating energy on them, a more compassionate air will prevail in your communication, and you will be better equipped to make progress. As well as using this spell, make sure to use your voice to educate rationally.

YOU WILL NEED

- Bunch of dried lavender
- Lighter or matches
- Small bowl
- Quiet, outdoor place to meditate

TIMING

Since this is a healing spell, meant to bring in understanding, it is best performed during a new or waxing moon. Air moons are recommended for this spell, as they deal with communication and intellect.

INSTRUCTIONS

1. Begin by casting your protective grid around you and your tools, then begin to ground and anchor into the earth.

2. Take the bunch of dried lavender and light it at one end, making it smoke. Place the bowl underneath to catch any falling pieces of herb. Always make sure to practice fire safety.

3. Use your smoldering lavender to draw a pentagram in the air, visualizing its power.

4. Place the lavender in the bowl and let it continue to smolder as you get into a comfortable position to meditate.

5. Begin to soften your gaze and finally close your eyes, sinking into a deep meditation while focusing on your breath. Breathe deeply in and out.

6. Once you have found a rhythmic pace for your breathing, begin to envision a soft, glowing, blue light emanating from your throat.

7. As you picture this light, let it grow with each repeated breath.

8. Once you have grown your light as big and bright as you can, take that light and send it to your intended subject. If the light is for you, keep it held in your mind's eye. If it is for the collective, send it out into the universe. If it is for someone in particular, imagine their throat glowing blue, too.

9. Continue to hold this visualization for as long as it is comfortable.

10. Once you feel the spell is complete, close your grid in whichever way feels good to you (see page 56).

WALK A MILE IN MY SHOES CHARM

This spell is intended to enlighten your subject. Instead of wishing for an illumination of thought, it shows by example. It is inspired by Hot Foot Powder (see pages 88-89), but rather than being used to drive out harmful subjects, it aims to have them experience a day in the life of someone who they simply can't relate to.

YOU WILL NEED
- 1 tbsp dried calendula
- 1 tbsp ground ginger
- 1 tbsp table salt
- 1 tbsp dried rosemary
- 1 tbsp dried lavender
- Mixing bowl
- Photograph of your subject
- Crossroads

TIMING
As this spell is for healing, I recommend new and waxing moons. Since herbs are used, and due to the physical manifestation of this spell, I recommend Earth moons as well.

EVEN JUST ONE DAY OF EXPERIENCING SOMEONE ELSE'S PAIN CAN MAKE A HUGE DIFFERENCE. WHILE THIS IS STILL TECHNICALLY A HEALING SPELL, THE HEALING IS CREATED BY REMOVING IGNORANCE, AND THAT CAN BE SOMEWHAT INTENSE IF THE SUBJECT IS NOT EXPECTING IT.

INSTRUCTIONS

1. Begin by grounding in your preferred way with all of your ingredients at hand.

2. First, add the ingredients, one by one, to the mixing bowl. As you add them, state the intention of each herb:

"Calendula to activate me as the healer."

"Ginger to ease anger and frustration."

"Salt to protect and cleanse."

"Rosemary to clear unwanted thoughts."

"And lavender to quiet the ego."

3. When all the ingredients have been added, begin mixing them together with your hand, channeling your intention directly into them. As you mix, imagine your subject feeling exactly what it is like to walk a mile in your shoes.

4. Once everything is mixed to your liking, take your photograph and the mixing bowl, then head out to a crossroads.

5. Take the photograph of your subject and place it on the ground at the crossroads. This does not have to be in the center, where you could get injured, but at a corner instead. You can use the easternmost corner to associate it with the Earth.

6. Place the photograph on the ground, then begin sprinkling the mixture on top. As you douse your subject, state again the intention to have your subject understand you. Make sure that your photograph is sufficiently covered.

7. When you have finished, say a quick "Thank you" to the spirits of the crossroads who will help to carry your intention to fruition.

8. Leave the photograph in place. If you have any mixture left, make sure to dispose of it outside your home.

HEALING BATH

For this spell you are going to use yourself as the vessel for a potion to send out healing into the world. Meditative baths have been used in witchcraft for centuries, and you can make your own quite easily. This spell will walk you through the steps for making your own healing stew.

If you do not have a bathtub, you can modify this spell by creating the mixture in a basin that you take into the shower with you. You then anoint yourself with the mixture by pouring it over your head and letting your body marinate in the ingredients.

YOU WILL NEED
- Bathtub or basin
- ½ cup chamomile flowers
- ½ cup pink Himalayan salt
- ½ cup rose petals
- ½ cup linden flowers
- ½ cup tulsi (holy basil) leaves

TIMING:
To give and express healing, this spell is best performed on a new moon, but a waxing moon will do the job too. Since this spell is intended for a bath/shower, and is very emotional and immersive, I suggest using Water moons, specifically Cancer, as they guard the home.

THE INTENTION FOR THIS BATH IS TO SEND OUT HEALING TO THE WORLD. IF YOU ARE IN NEED OF HEALING YOURSELF, ADJUST YOUR INTENTION AS DESIRED.

INSTRUCTIONS

1. Begin by collecting your tools and bringing them into the bathroom/shower with you.

2. If you are modifying this spell for the shower, premix all your dry ingredients in the basin. Then you can add water to anoint yourself once you get in the shower.

3. Run your bath at lukewarm temperature. Lukewarm baths tend to work better energetically than very hot ones, but you should use your intuition if you feel guided in another direction.

4. Slowly add the ingredients to the bath as it fills, stating your intention to heal.

5. Once your bath is full and your ingredients are added, get into the bath and cast your protective grid around you.

6. As you soak, sink into a meditative state by doing a body scan (see page 42), starting from the top of your head and moving all the way down to the tips of your toes, feeling and releasing any tenseness.

7. Once you have scanned your body and are in a state of comfort, access your heart's center by beginning to grow a green light in your chest. Channel how comfortable you are into the universe, and direct your comfort to others.

8. As you are channeling, focusing, and growing your green light, take the herbs in the bath and anoint your body with them wherever it feels good to do so. You can follow the points from the Crystal Grid Visualization (see pages 54-57), or simply follow your intuition.

9. If you are in the shower, pour the premixed ingredients in the basin over your head as you wash yourself, rubbing them over your body while you relax and send out a loving energy.

10. Bathe or shower for as long as your intuition tells you to. When you are ready, soften the light of your heart's center and begin to come back to a more alert state.

11. If you are in the bath, let the water drain away while you are still in it.

12. Close and send your protective grid up into the universe. Do not rinse off the mixture for 24 hours, and throw the discarded ingredients outside your home.

NATIONWIDE HEALING POTION

For this spell, you are going to cast a large amount of energy to heal the nation from whichever tragedy you have chosen to direct your intention toward. Unfortunately, there are many to choose from, but it is wise to pick one at a time and stick with it, as general intentions will get lost in the shuffle. Make sure to be specific about what you wish to heal, so that the universe can direct it effectively.

This spell is created in a cauldron, so get ready to flex your witchiest muscles! If you do not have a proper cauldron readily available, you can use a cooking pot that is consecrated for spellwork—I use one and it works just fine.

YOU WILL NEED
- Cauldron or cooking pot
- Pen and paper
- 1 tsp ground cinnamon
- 1 tbsp dried dandelion
- 1 tbsp tulsi
(holy basil) leaves
- Lighter or matches
- White vinegar

TIMING
This spell is great to set the intention for protection, so new and waxing moons are ideal.

INSTRUCTIONS

1. Grab your tools first and clear out a safe space to work.

2. Begin by casting your protective grid around you and your pen and paper, then begin to ground.

3. Once you have a comfortable spot where you feel secure, take your pen and paper and write out your intention. Remember to be specific.

4. Sprinkle your paper with the cinnamon to signify quick healing. Fold the paper three times away from you to send your intention out. Then light a corner of the paper and drop it into your cauldron or pot. Make sure to practice fire safety.

5. Sprinkle the dandelion and tulsi on top of the flame. These herbs are great for healing grief.

6. As your ingredients burn, meditate on sending out healing. Let the fragrance permeate your space with its healing scent, and inhale strength and exhale compassion.

7. Continue to meditate for as long as it feels good. When you are ready, wake yourself out of your meditation by clapping your hands once.

8. You may now close your protective grid, and send the energy up into the universe.

9. Toss the ingredients outside your home, and wash your cauldron or pot with white vinegar to cleanse it. Keep the vessel in a safe space and use it only for spellwork.

WRITE YOUR OWN SPELLS

Now that you have seen how spells are structured, and understand the basics of how and why to perform spellwork, you can begin to create your own spells! Witchcraft is a craft, after all, so think of each spell as an art project, using it to amplify your intention.

I have compiled a comprehensive list of ingredients, deities, moon phases, and more that can each be energetically matched to whichever intention you choose. Think of this process as an outfit—you can mix and match as you see fit. However, there is no need to oversaturate your spells with every ingredient you can find. You do not need any, as a matter of fact.

In witchcraft, your intention is the most powerful ingredient, and everything else is an accessory. Your intention must be strong to start with, and the ingredients then simply expand and radiate the energy due to their own innate power. With experience, you will grow your intuition and decide what works best for you, as your own, empowered, witchy self.

SPELL CRAFT

Follow this simple structure:

SET THE INTENTION

Before you begin any type of spellwork, you should have a very clear idea of what you wish to manifest into existence. This is called an intention. If you have done your due diligence and explored the spells in this book, you should already be familiar with this concept.

1

CRAFT

Now, you are going to craft your spell. This means designing it with whatever ritual, performance, and ingredients you think best fit your intention. Obviously, it is much better to begin spellwork knowing what you plan to do, so that you can focus all your energy on bringing your intention into existence rather than scrambling around at the last minute.

2

GROUND

Grounding is an essential step, as it anchors you energetically while you work with higher spirits. It brings you "down to earth," so to speak. There are many ways to practice grounding (see page 40), but a very easy way to perform this step is to imagine roots growing down from your feet and into the earth, quite literally rooting you down.

PROTECT

Do not skip this step, as it is meant to keep you safe. While you do not have to cast a circle or even a protective grid (see pages 54-57), you should always practice some form of energetic cleansing and protection before you begin spell casting. There are many forces at work when you perform this type of magic, and protection is key.

CAST

Now you are ready to cast! With your intention in your mind's eye and your spell designed, this is where you can perform your spell or ritual. The reason why this step is almost last is because spellwork lies more in the preparation than it does in the actual casting, so make sure to have taken proper care in the former.

THANK

After casting your spell, close whatever protection you invoked, then thank the universe just as you would thank a friend for a favor. You may also thank any specific deities you work closely with, or just thank spirits in general for protecting you and carrying out the spell. This is essential, as it forges a relationship with unseen forces.

HOW TO CRAFT YOUR INTENTION

Intention is the single most powerful tool at a witch's disposal. There is a method for crafting an intention, so here I will show you exactly how to create one that sticks.

THE WHO, WHAT, WHERE, WHEN, AND WHY

When you create an intention, it is important to first identify the who, what, where, when, and why associated with your desire. Although the who is very important because it involves thinking through the ethics and reason behind your hex—which means you have to decide whether your target truly deserves to be hexed—for other spellwork the "who" is often yourself!

Next, you should identify what you would like the who to transform into with this energetic working. If a "where" is applicable, this should also be identified, so the universe knows where to direct its will. Timing may also be a factor, and in this

case, "when" is important. However, I would advise that you surrender to this concept, as the universe has the final ruling.

Finally, the most important part of your intention exists in the "why." You must know exactly why you wish to cast, otherwise you will be blindly throwing energy, and that is not casting with integrity. If this aspect of hexing is difficult for you, I advise you go back to the drawing board.

TRY TO BE SPECIFIC

Now that you have the basics of your intention in place, see if you can get even more specific. The chances are, if you've followed the instructions above carefully, you should already have a fairly precise idea of what you intend. However, rather than a "who" being "all disenfranchised people," for example, you could get more specific by saying: "those disenfranchised people who are experiencing ___" and go deeper still.

There are many base thoughts and beliefs being thrown around at any given moment. So, the more specific you can be with your intetion, the higher the chances that it will land successfully.

BE DIRECT

It is also important to be direct when stating your intention. This is not the time to skirt around details; use this time to make your intention land like a spear rather than waft like a paper airplane. For example, it is more efficient to say "Heal my family from toxic ancestral ties" than "Make my family stop saying toxic things" because it gets straight to the root of the problem.

KEEP THE INTENTION POSITIVE

Finally, many practitioners believe that an intention needs to be kept positive. Here, I am not necessarily referring to the contents of the intention, but rather to how it is phrased. For instance, I find that the word "no" is an extremely powerful form of magic, but, following the principle of direct and specific intentions, it is more powerful to say "Keep my home protected from violence" than "No more violence is permitted in my home."

CHOOSING THE RIGHT COMPONENTS

When crafting a spell, you may want to accessorize your intention with ingredients that will amplify what you are trying to get across. Everything has energy, and in crafting your spells you will want to find energetic complements for your intentions.

For example, if your intention is "Protect me from outside harm and bring me clarity to see when it is coming," you will want to consider a few things.

Protection is a big factor in this intention, so you should look for components that will increase the protective energy. Listed toward the end of this chapter, you will find herbs and stones, for example, that contain this type of protective vibration and will help support your spell. Some protective components are more specific than others, so, depending on what fits your intention, you can choose whether to incorporate them. In this case, as you need protection from outside harm rather than your own inner thoughts, you may want to choose obsidian (a protective barrier stone) rather than amethyst (a stone that neutralizes thoughts).

Another factor to consider is clarity, so peruse this chapter for components that provide this as well. As you read through this section of the book, it will become obvious what fits and what does not.

The reason for using these components is rather like souping up a car with add-ons and accessories. It doesn't necessarily make the car drive any better or faster, but it does make the ride more pleasant and the energetic vibe of the ride higher. In this example, your intention is the car, your focused energy is the gas, and those sweet leather seats and the GPS navigation system are the components you choose.

That being said, these accessories are not needed. Simply wishing and focusing on your intention can be enough to manifest it into existence. But by using these extra tools, you may be provided with energetic assistance as a newbie to hexing.

MOON PHASES

The Moon is a very powerful ally when you are casting spells. Many witches design their life around the cycle of the Moon, aligning their practice to suit whichever phase or astrological sign the Moon is in on a given day. However, if you do not feel aligned with the Moon, it is not mandatory that you abide by this.

Over the course of 29.5 days, the Moon moves from looking completely dark, slowly becoming brighter until it is full, to receiving the entire reflection of the Sun before shrinking again, back to a new Moon. Each of these phases has a different type of energy, and as the Moon is small and circles the Earth quickly, it also transits the astrological signs approximately every three days. Use this section to determine which phases of the Moon are most appropriate for your spells.

NEW MOON

WAXING MOON

FULL MOON

New This is the start of the cycle, when the Moon has no light and is beginning to grow. As the Moon is essentially an empty vessel for the light of the Sun, and its light is so full of potential, it is said that this phase is best to set an intention to manifest. This phase will help you bring in what you desire. This phase lasts about three days.

Waxing This is the period between the new and full moons, when the light grows. As the **Moon** fills with the light of the Sun, this is an excellent phase for nourishing your intention. This helps to bring in what you have set in motion continuously. This phase lasts around 11 days.

Full This phase is the apex of light in the Moon. Everyone at some point in their life has marveled at the light of a full moon—it is a phenomenon that is hard to ignore. Because the light has reached its climax,

this is an excellent phase to assess your intention, and see what has worked and what hasn't. This stage marks the top of the rollercoaster—from here the light will start fading, making it a good time for reflection. This phase lasts about three days.

Waning The light of the Moon begins to fade during this phase. As the light diminishes, so do our attachments. From here, witches like to focus on releasing and banishing negative energy. This phase lasts about 11 days.

Dark This phase is suitable for banishing and hexing. It is the final phase of the waning moon, lasting only about one day before the next new moon. In this phase you'll find that dark magic has extra oomph.

Note: You can use the Internet to find the Moon phases for your specific location.

WANING MOON

DARK MOON

ASTROLOGY

Whether you feel aligned to work with astrology or not, there are always energetic influences in the sky that make an impact on our daily behaviors. Personally, I like to use the entire cosmology of the stars to craft my spellwork, but for beginners (since this is a very dense subject) focusing on the Sun and the Moon with these energies will help to guide you in effective timing. Whenever the Sun is in a certain astrological sign, it will use this energy as the overall vibe. When the Moon is in a certain astrological sign, however, its undertones and shadow tendencies will be influenced.

Aries The first sign of the zodiac begins with a bang. This sign is an independent Fire sign that brings creativity and self-sufficiency.

Taurus This Earth sign is grounded and rooted in the material. It is the sign of comfort and luxury, and great for manifestation.

Gemini Chatty Gemini is great for opening up communication as it is an Air sign. It also has a dual nature, so use this influence when you need to see two sides or play two roles.

Cancer Being an emotional Water sign who loves the home, this sign is like the mama bear of the zodiac. I like using this energy for protection.

Libra The Air sign of relationships (platonic and otherwise), this romantic sign encourages thinking of the "other" rather than of the "self."

Capricorn Hard-working Capricorn is an Earth sign dedicated to career and reputation. This is another excellent energy to manifest under.

Leo Party-starter Leo is a Fire sign that brings play, fun, and flirtation to the mix. However, it is also the lion who is ruled by the heart, so this energy is big on abundance.

Scorpio This sexy and transformative Water sign influences deep intimacy. As the detective of the zodiac, this sign knows how to get to the bottom of any situation.

Aquarius This Air sign is most concerned with the collective, so use this energy in order to do social-justice work!

Virgo This Earth sign is the sign of service and practical self-care. Think scheduling doctor's appointments and making sure to drink plenty of water. It isn't glamorous, but someone has to do it!

Sagittarius Expansive Sagittarius is a Fire sign that shoots for the truth. This type of energy is excellent for matters of a philosophical nature.

Pisces As the final sign of the zodiac, this Water sign marks endings and transformation. Use this energy to seriously get in touch with your emotions.

CANDLE COLORS

Candles have long been used by witches, far before pop culture adorned movie sets with elaborate candelabras. The power of candles comes from the flickering flame and the smoke (if any) provided by the candle. You can tell a lot about your candle magic by paying attention to the behavior of the flame.

For example, if your flame is burning high and steady, you can surmise that your spell is working well. However, if your flame is flickering and chaotic, you may glean from this that there is an additional block to your magic, which must be addressed. Use your intuition as you create a relationship with your flame to better understand what it is telling you.

In addition, color magic is based on the principle that every color has an energetic vibration. If we match these vibrations with candles, we can add an additional amplifier to our candle magic. Here are the correspondences for each candle color:

Black Great for protection and banishment. Its dark hue is the presence of all colors, and is able to absorb any negativity.

White Good for any type of magic. As white is the absence of all color, it is absolutely pure.

Purple Enhances intuition and connects to both your crown and third eye chakras. It is also associated with luxury and royalty.

Blue A great color for communication and also opening your throat chakra. Also associated with the element of Water, blue can have a great calming effect.

Green As the color of money, green is perfect for amplifying abundance. Lesser known for its love-magic abilities, it also helps to open up your heart chakra.

Yellow The color of joy and the color of the Sun, yellow is great for increasing happiness. Yellow is also associated with your solar plexus, increased confidence, and the Air element, which is excellent for increasing positive thoughts.

Orange This color is associated with your sacral chakra, and helps to amplify creativity. I burn an orange candle whenever I experience writer's block.

Red Passion is the name of the game for red. This sexy color increases lust and desire, and also adds a passionate element to creative projects.

Gold Said to be masculine, gold is associated with the Sun. It is also the color of lavish abundance.

Silver Said to be feminine, the color silver is associated with the Moon. It is also very protective.

HERBS

Herbs are another excellent way to enhance your spellwork. You can burn herbs, "dress" your candles by coating them with herbs, or put them in an amulet—the options are endless!

Here are some of my favorite herbs to work with, which can all be found at any grocery store. I prefer to work with dried herbs, as they burn better and keep for longer. If you would like to dry your own herbs, buy them fresh and wash them, then place in the oven on the lowest setting for a few minutes while monitoring them to ensure they do not burn. This will dry them out and ensure that there are no extra pesticides or additives on the herbs you are using.

Sage Aside from the overharvested Native American white sage that is sold in bundles for smoke clearing, European (or common) sage can be used just as well! Sage is great for cleansing, blessing the home, redemption, and prosperity.

Rosemary This can be used for protection, strength, and cleansing, but it is also great for improving memory.

Clove Wonderfully aromatic, clove is great for banishing evil, providing protection, and healing physical pain. If made in a tea, it's known to dull toothache.

Rose This common flower is best known for its ability to amplify romance. However, it can also be used to ward off the evil eye (see page 21).

Cinnamon One of my favorite herbs to use, cinnamon speeds up spells and amplifies success and victory. This is equally great for abundance and hexing.

Basil This herb is great for protection and exorcism, as well as abundance in both love and money. It all depends on your intention.

Thyme Using thyme in spells is excellent for enhancing strength, courage, and a positive attitude. It's a wonderful accessory for any spell.

Lavender Lavender has a range of gifts, from banishing harmful spirits to purification to increasing intelligence.

STONES

Crystals are a big favorite among novice witches and seasoned practitioners alike. These Earth-made stones have been collecting energy for millions of years and carry an ancient vibration that is unique to each of them. Whether you are meditating with a stone or using it to amplify a spell, the magic of crystals is very apparent. Here are a few of my go-tos:

Black obsidian This stone is my absolute favorite because (in my humble opinion) it is the best for protecting against ill will. I often use this stone when working because it keeps me safe from others projecting (knowingly or not) their fears onto me.

Black tourmaline Another great protection stone, this works best with lower-level, unintentional, negative energy. This stone is best worn in social situations.

Garnet This is an excellent stone for passion. Its fire is extremely potent.

Amethyst This is a great stone for clarity and mental stability. You can also use this stone by tucking it under your pillow for more effective dream work and even lucid dreaming.

Clear quartz This quartz is essentially an amplifier of amplifiers. It adds clarity to a situation and connects to your crown chakra, but it also serves as a magnifier for other ingredients.

Jasper This stone is excellent for stress and sucking the anxiety out of a situation. It's great for leveling you out so you can cast an effective spell. It also absorbs negative energy, so you receive both protection from yourself and others!

Rose quartz The "It girl" of crystals at the moment, rose quartz is nothing to scoff at. This stone is a self-love amplifier and, quite simply, when we love ourselves, nothing can stand in our way.

Labradorite One of my favorite stones, this crystal is great for protection against psychic attacks, but also key in maintaining personal strength and power during times of transformation.

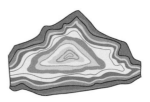

Agate Another great stone that transforms negative energy, and also improves mental competence and concentration. Agate helps to shift perceptions, making it a good choice to work with alongside this book.

DEITIES

Working with deities, as with any other components in this chapter, is not necessary if you want to be a witch. However, deities are very powerful forces, and invoking their energy can have a massive impact when you are casting spells.

Think of calling on a deity like asking a friend for a favor; it would be a really silly move not to give thanks or to respect and appreciate their time. You can do so by putting out a glass of water, simply by saying "Please" and "Thank you," or by offering something the deity enjoys. If you are offering something that can spoil, make sure to discard it outside your home after you've worked your magic.

IT IS IMPORTANT TO NOTE, HOWEVER, THAT WHEN YOU WORK WITH A DEITY, YOU NEED TO GIVE THANKS AND RESPECT THEIR ENERGY.

Kali India's most prominent warrior goddess, Kali is depicted with eight arms and an outstretched tongue, and also wearing a belt of the heads of her enemies. She is strong; she is a conqueror. Use her energy wisely because once she is summoned, she gets a job done. You can offer Kali red hibiscus flowers (don't smell these, as the offering is meant for her) or her favorite tool in battle—a knife.

Freyja A Norse goddess who is not only a warrior, but also a love goddess, Freyja certainly has range. She is known for helping soldiers in battle cross over to the other side, and is also believed to increase fertility. Freyja rides on a chariot led by two cats and wears a coat of falcon feathers. She enjoys a glass of mead as an offering.

Athena The Greek goddess of strategic warfare, mathematics, and strength, Athena is a very intelligent deity to summon. Offering Athena olive oil is a great way to honor her.

Bast The Egyptian cat goddess, Bast, or Bastet, governs health and healing. She is also very protective of humans against contagious diseases and evil spirits. You can offer catnip to Bast if you want to work with her.

The Morrigan Hailing from Ireland, The Morrigan is a trinity goddess who is associated with the crow. As a goddess of death, rebirth, and beauty, you should offer The Morrigan red wine or red meat if you want to work with her.

Hekate The Greek goddess of magic and witchcraft, Hekate (or Hecate), is excellent to work with when carrying out any type of mysticism, but most notably in work with the dead. In order to work with her, give her an offering of honey or fish.

Huitzilopochtli For some masculine energy, the Aztec god of war and the Sun Huitzilopochtli is great to work with when commanding peace through sacrfice. Offer him turquoise or a bird's feather to work with him.

Thor In Germanic lore, Thor wields his hammer for protection in battle. As another dominant masculine deity, offer him ale or even a household hammer to work with him.

INDEX

Published by Chicago Review Press Incorporated
814 North Franklin Street
Chicago, Illinois 60610

© 2020 Quarto Publishing plc,
an imprint of The Quarto Group

All illustrations by Olya Kamieshkova (based on the original illustration package
Complete Mystica Collection by Elevens – Autumn Hutchins) with the
exception of: page 11 Science History Images / Alamy Stock Photo; page 19
Magica / Alamy Stock Photo; page 23 c/o Michael M. Hughes (Magic for the
Resistance: Rituals and Spells for Change), artwork by Karina Ruiz Diaz.

ISBN 978-1-64160-448-2

10 9 8 7 6 5 4 3 2 1

QUAR.336381

Art Director: Gemma Wilson
Designer: Clare Barber
Illustrations: Olya Kamieshkova
Copy Editor: Caroline West
Editor: Emma Harverson
Publisher: Samantha Warrington

Printed in Singapore

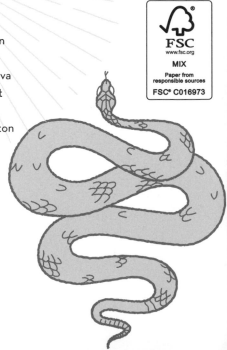

FSC
www.fsc.org
MIX
Paper from
responsible sources
FSC® C016973